POKÉMON™

MY POKÉMON COOKBOOK

Delicious Recipes Inspired by Pikachu and Friends

POKÉMON™

MY POKÉMON COOKBOOK

Delicious Recipes Inspired by Pikachu and Friends

Victoria Rosenthal

INSIGHT EDITIONS
San Rafael • Los Angeles • London

Contents

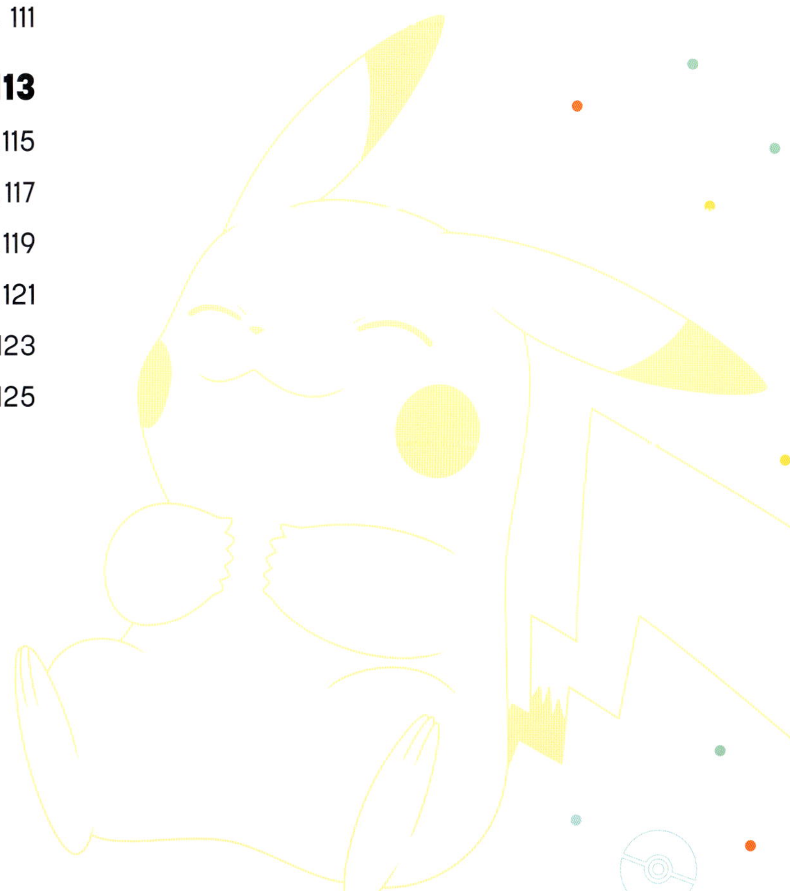

Introduction

The world of Pokémon is a story of adventure, friendship, and being the very best you can be. Although the goal is typically about forming the strongest team of Pokémon you can and defeating the reigning champion to claim the title for yourself, being the new Pokémon champion isn't possible without forming friendships and true bonds on the way. The charm of the journey is universal.

The goal of this cookbook is to take that love of Pokémon that so many people share and extend it to the wonderful world of cuisine. These recipes include all sorts of drinks, desserts, and other delicious dishes that celebrate and cherish all the amazing varieties of Pokémon out there, taking inspiration from all the different types of Pokémon to think of great ways to get in the kitchen and get cooking. We can come up with Fire-type dishes that are spicy and warm you up. Electric-type dishes full of sour elements that bring a spark to your plate. Ground-type dishes that are filling and dense, and eating too much may leave you, well, grounded for a time. Each and every known type is represented in this cookbook, and I hope you enjoy the characteristics that show themselves in the meals they are tied to!

All of the recipes in this book are family friendly. Pokémon has fans of all ages, and another goal of this book is to bring the family into the kitchen and combine a love of Pokémon with a love of food. This book provides fun ways to bring those less familiar with culinary adventures into the kitchen. There are a few more complicated recipes that will require extra care and a helping hand, but there are also plenty of meals that are easily approachable for anyone new to cooking.

So let's get cooking! There are lots of fun treats and tasty dishes to enjoy. Now you can cook them all and perhaps even make some friends along the way.

Ingredient Guide

Aburaage are thinly sliced, deep-fried tofu pockets used in Japanese cuisine.

Blue spirulina is an extract from spirulina, a type of microalgae. For the recipes in this book, you will want to use the powder variety of this ingredient.

Butterfly pea flowers are dried flowers that grow in Southeast Asia. The flower is dehydrated and commonly used for tea. It is used to dye things a bright blue color.

Calabrian chile peppers are smoky chile peppers grown in Italy. They have a Scoville scale rating between 25,000 and 40,000 SHU.

Chinese five-spice powder is a combination of cinnamon, Szechuan peppercorns, star anise, fennel seeds, and cloves. It can be stored in the pantry for up to a year, but keep in mind that spices will lose their flavor the longer they are stored.

Condensed milk is milk that has been gently heated, had 60 percent of the water removed, been mixed with sugar, and canned. This is an extremely thick, caramelized sweetened milk. It is typically found in cans that can be stored in the pantry for about a year. Once opened, it must be refrigerated and used within 2 weeks.

Evaporated milk is milk that has been gently heated and had 60 percent of the water removed to make a dense, creamy milk. It is found in cans that can be stored in a pantry for about 6 months. Once opened, it must be refrigerated and used within 5 days.

Gochujang is a Korean thick chile paste that contains red chile peppers, sticky rice, fermented soybeans, and sweeteners. Heat levels of gochujang can vary and are displayed on the container with a spice indicator. Once gochujang is opened, it must be stored in an airtight container in the refrigerator.

Hoisin sauce is a sweet, thick sauce used in Chinese cuisine, especially BBQ, made from fermented soybean and Chinese five-spice powder. It can be used for cooking or just as a dipping sauce. Hoisin sauce can be stored in the pantry until opened. Once opened, store in a refrigerator.

Kashmiri chile powder is made from the Kashmiri chile that has been dried and ground. Kashmiri chile has a mild heat with a vibrant red coloring. A good substitute for Kashmiri chile powder includes paprika or another mild chile.

Miso is a Japanese paste made from fermented soybeans. Miso comes in several varieties including white (the mildest flavor) and red (allowed to age for longer, making it saltier and with a stronger flavor). Miso can be stored in an airtight container in the refrigerator.

Nori is a dried edible sheet of seaweed used in Japanese cuisine. It is most commonly used to wrap sushi rolls. Nori can be stored in a cool pantry.

Plantains are related to bananas but are much starchier and can't be eaten raw. Unripe plantains will be green in color. As they ripen, they turn yellow (medium) and eventually black (fully ripe).

Rice paper is a super thin wrapper made from rice and used in Vietnamese cuisine. The sheets are dry and need to be rehydrated before use as a wrapper.

Strawberry powder is dehydrated strawberries that have been blended into a powder. You can find this product easily online, or you can use dehydrated strawberries that you grind into a fine powder with a food processor.

Thai basil is an herb with purple stems and green leaves used in Southeast Asian cuisine. It has a licorice-like and mildly spicy flavor. It is a slightly sturdier herb than Italian basil and is more stable at higher cooking temperatures. Thai basil can be substituted with any type of basil, but it will have a different flavor profile.

Tonkatsu sauce is a thick, sweet sauce used in Japanese cuisine. It can be stored in the pantry. Once opened, it can be stored in the refrigerator in an airtight container for about two months.

Umeboshi are pickled plums used in Japanese cuisine. They are extremely sour and salty.

Vanilla Beans are commonly used to flavor recipes by slicing them open and scraping the insides. You can substitute 1 tablespoon of vanilla extract or vanilla paste per bean.

Vital wheat gluten is wheat flour that has had most of its starch removed, leaving the wheat proteins behind. The protein content is between 75 and 85 percent. Adding it to a dough will yield a much more elastic and chewier texture.

Allergy Notes

Just like how all Pokémon have their own strengths and weaknesses, people have their own personal tastes and food restrictions. It is important when cooking that you are ready to make adjustments in order to avoid any food allergies. Keep in mind restrictions and accommodations for yourself and any guests you may be feeding. It's always fine to make adjustments to fit the recipes to your own needs.

Adapting to Vegetarian Diets

Most of the recipes in this book are vegetarian or vegan friendly. The remaining two recipes can be adapted to your dietary needs. Swap out proteins with your favorite grilled vegetable or meat substitute. This will affect the cooking times, so plan ahead. Many of the vegetarian dishes can also be adjusted to become vegan by simply using dairy or honey alternatives.

Adapting to Gluten-Free Diets

For most recipes, you can use equal ratios of gluten substitute for flour, but be prepared to modify the quantity just in case the consistency seems off compared to how they are described in the recipes.

Adapting to Lactose-Free Diets

Feel free to replace milk and heavy cream with your favorite nondairy milk. There are also plenty of butter alternatives that work well to replace butter in recipes. Replacing butter with oil isn't always the best choice, as it doesn't give the same consistency needed for certain recipes. If you do use oil instead, add it in smaller batches to check the consistency as you go.

Poké Ball
Dusk Ball
Fast Ball

Poké Ball Poke Bowls

Poké Balls come in a tremendous variety, but they are all useful in the right circumstances. A Pokémon Trainer needs to be prepared, so let's look at a few ways to prepare our own poke bowls as well. Try making your favorite Poké Ball shapes with some of your favorite ingredients!

Difficulty: ●●○○
Prep Time: 45 minutes
Rest Time: 1 hour
Cook Time: 15 minutes
Yield: 6 servings
Dietary Notes:
- **Poké Ball & Fast Ball:** Nondairy
- **Dusk Ball:** Vegan

Equipment: Rice cooker, cutting board, knife, small nonstick pan, bowls

Sushi Rice

4 cups (840 grams) sushi rice
Water
2 tablespoons (30 milliliters) rice vinegar
1 tablespoon (15 grams) sugar
½ teaspoon (2 grams) kosher salt

note: Make sure to follow the ratios of your rice cooker. Measure with the cup it came with and add the amount of water it recommends.

Poké Ball

2 tablespoons (30 milliliters) soy sauce
2 teaspoons (10 milliliters) sesame oil
1 teaspoon (5 milliliters) rice vinegar
1 teaspoon (2 grams) grated fresh ginger
1 scallion, white and light green parts finely chopped
12 ounces (340 grams) sushi-grade tuna, cubed
¼ to ½ portion of the cooked sushi rice
1 sheet nori

Sushi Rice

1. Put rice in a bowl, fill it up with cold water, and rub in a circular motion. The water will become opaque, which means it still needs to be cleaned. Strain the water out and repeat until the water is clear.
2. Place the cleaned rice and the amount of water required into a rice cooker and allow the rice to cook.
3. When the rice is done cooking, remove from the rice cooker and place inside a nonmetallic bowl.
4. In a small bowl, combine rice vinegar, sugar, and salt. Add the vinegar mixture to the rice while the rice is still hot. Take a rice paddle and fold in the rice vinegar. Continue to fold and slice the rice until it has cooled down.

Poké Ball

1. Combine the soy sauce, sesame oil, rice vinegar, ginger, and scallions in an airtight container. Whisk together until well combined. Add the tuna and stir to combine. Seal the container and place in the refrigerator. Let tuna rest in the refrigerator for 30 minutes, up to 1 hour.
2. To serve, take two bowls and place a serving of sushi rice in each. Top the top half of each with the tuna. Use a piece of nori to create the black line in the center of the Poké Ball.

Equipment: Rice cooker, cutting board, knife, small nonstick pan, bowls

Dusk Ball

1 pound (454 grams) seedless watermelon, cubed

3 tablespoons (45 milliliters) soy sauce

1 lime, zested and juiced

2 teaspoons (10 milliliters) sesame oil

2 teaspoons (10 milliliters) rice vinegar

1 teaspoon (2 grams) grated fresh ginger

1 teaspoon (2 grams) sugar

¼ to ½ portion of the cooked sushi rice

½ cup (80 grams) edamame

1 avocado, thinly sliced

1 sheet nori

Fast Ball

2 tablespoons (30 milliliters) soy sauce

2 teaspoons (10 milliliters) sesame oil

1 teaspoon (5 milliliters) rice vinegar

1 teaspoon (2 grams) grated fresh ginger

1 scallion, white and light green parts finely chopped

12 ounces (340 grams) sushi-grade salmon, cubed

¼ to ½ portion of the cooked sushi rice

1 mango, peeled and thinly sliced

1 sheet nori

Dusk Ball

1. Heat a small nonstick pan over medium heat. Add the watermelon and cook until it is no longer releasing liquid, about 5 to 8 minutes. Remove from the heat and allow to cool completely.

2. Combine the soy sauce, lime juice and zest, sesame oil, rice vinegar, ginger, and sugar in an airtight container. Whisk together until well combined. Add the watermelon and stir to combine. Seal the container and place in the refrigerator. Let the watermelon rest in the refrigerator for at least 1 hour, but overnight is best.

3. To serve, take two bowls and place a serving of sushi rice in each. Cover the top half of each with edamame. Cover the bottom half with sliced avocado. Use a piece of shaped nori to create the black lines of the Dusk Ball. Finally, place a row of watermelon in the center.

Fast Ball

1. Combine the soy sauce, sesame oil, rice vinegar, ginger, and scallions in an airtight container. Whisk together until well combined. Add the salmon and stir to combine. Seal the container and place in the refrigerator. Let salmon rest in the refrigerator for 30 minutes, up to 1 hour.

2. To serve, take two bowls and place a serving of sushi rice in each. Top the top half of each with the salmon. Place slices of mango on the sides to make the Fast Ball. Use a piece of nori to create the black line in the center.

Kanto Region

Charizard

Pikachu

Gengar

Seaking

Dragonite

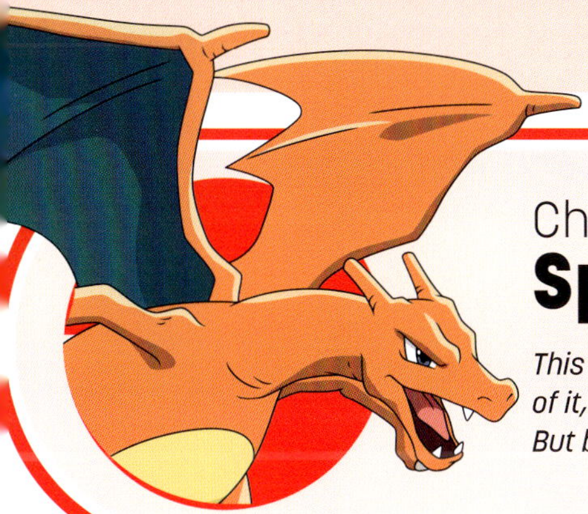

Charizard

Spicy Arrabbiata

This spicy arrabbiata is full of flavor and heat. Eat enough of it, and you may be able to blow flames just like Charizard! But breathe fire carefully if you do.

Difficulty: ●○○○
Prep Time: 30 minutes
Cook Time: 45 minutes
Yield: 4 servings
Dietary Notes: Vegetarian

Equipment: Large nonstick pan, large pot, cutting board, knife, cheese grater

3 tablespoons (45 milliliters) olive oil
5 garlic cloves, minced
2 tablespoons (28 grams) tomato paste
1 teaspoon (5 grams) sweet paprika
1 teaspoon (2 grams) dried chile flakes
4 to 6 Calabrian chile peppers, chopped
1 large lemon, zested
One 28-ounce (794-gram) can San Marzano tomatoes
2 teaspoons (10 grams) sugar
¼ cup (25 grams) Pecorino Romano, shredded, plus more for serving
1 pound spaghetti, cooked and 1 cup water reserved
Kosher salt
Ground black pepper
¼ ounce (7 grams) fresh basil

1. Combine the olive oil, garlic, and tomato paste in a large nonstick pan. Heat over medium heat. Cook for 5 minutes until the garlic just starts to brown. Add the paprika, chile flakes, Calabrian chile peppers, and lemon zest.
2. Crush the San Marzano tomatoes with your hands and add them to the pan. Add the sugar and Pecorino Romano and mix everything together. Reduce the heat to medium-low and simmer for 30 minutes.
3. Add the cooked pasta and mix together. If too thick, add pasta water to loosen. Season with salt and pepper. Serve with fresh basil and extra Pecorino Romano.

Pikachu

Lemon Tart

These lemon tarts are the perfect dessert to enjoy with your best friends. You can't exchange electricity with friends like Pikachu can, but you can share these shockingly tart treats.

Difficulty: ●●○○
Prep Time: 1 hour
Rest Time: 3 hours
Cook Time: 30 minutes
Yield: 12 tarts
Dietary Notes: Vegetarian

Equipment: Food processor, 4-inch (10-centimeter) tart tins, rolling pin, large baking sheet, parchment paper, pie weights, medium saucepan, spatula, wire rack

Tart Shells

1½ cups (230 grams) all purpose flour
½ cup (68 grams) powdered sugar
½ teaspoon (2 grams) kosher salt
½ cup (112 grams) unsalted butter, cubed and chilled
2 egg yolks
1 tablespoon (6 grams) lemon zest
1 teaspoon (5 milliliters) vanilla extract
1 tablespoon (15 milliliters) milk

Lemon Curd

6 egg yolks
1¼ cups (250 grams) sugar
2 tablespoons (12 grams) lemon zest
$^{2}/_{3}$ cup (158 milliliters) lemon juice
1 pinch kosher salt
¾ cup (168 grams) unsalted butter
2 drops yellow food dye (optional)

For assembly

Fresh raspberries for decorating
White, black, and yellow candy melts for decorating

To make the tart shells

1. Combine flour, powdered sugar, and salt in a food processor. Add the cubed butter. Pulse until the mixture resembles coarse meal with a few chunks of butter.

2. Add the egg yolks, lemon zest, vanilla extract, and milk. Pulse until the dough comes together. Remove the dough from the food processor and lightly knead to bring it all together. Split into two portions. Wrap in plastic wrap and place in the refrigerator for at least 1 hour.

3. Take one of the dough portions and split it into 6 pieces. Take one of the pieces and roll it out to the size of your tart tin. Carefully lay the dough into the tin and remove any excess. Prick the bottom of the tart with a fork and place on a large baking sheet. Repeat with the remaining dough pieces. Place the baking sheet with the tarts in the freezer for 10 minutes before baking.

note: If you only have a few small tart tins, you can do this and the baking steps in smaller batches. Just make sure to leave any dough unused in the refrigerator until your tins are ready to use again.

4. Preheat oven to 375°F (191°C). Place a small piece of parchment paper on top of each of the crusts. Fill with pie weights (or dry beans) to help keep the crust from rising. Bake for 13 minutes.

5. Take the tarts out and remove the parchment paper and weights. Place back in the oven and bake until the crust is golden brown, about 3 to 5 minutes. Allow to cool slightly before removing from the tins and letting cool completely on a wire rack.

continued on the next page

To make the lemon curd

1. In a medium saucepan, whisk the egg yolks, sugar, and lemon zest until the sugar dissolves and smooths. Add the lemon juice and salt. Place over low heat and whisk until it becomes thick, about 10 minutes.

note: To test if the curd is thick enough, dip a spoon in the mixture and run a finger across the back of it. If the trail holds, it is okay! Keep in mind the curd will continue to thicken as it cools.

2. Add the butter and yellow food dye. Whisk until the butter is completely melted. Allow to cool for 10 minutes.

3. Carefully pour the curd into the cooled tart crust. If there are any major bubbles in the curd, use a toothpick to pop them. Place in a deep dish and cover, making sure the curd is not being touched by anything, so it doesn't stick as it cools.

4. Place in the refrigerator for at least 1 hour before serving. The curd can be refrigerated for up to 1 week.

5. Prepare a baking sheet with parchment paper. Begin by preparing the eyes. Place white candy melts in a pastry bag. Heat up in the microwave for 30 seconds to 1 minute, until the candy melt is melted.

6. Cut the end of the pastry bag and shape small white rounds for the white part of Pikachu's eye on the prepared parchment paper. Make 24 off these in total.

7. Place black candy melts in a pastry bag. Heat up in the microwave for 30 seconds to 1 minute, until the candy melt is melted.

8. Cut the end of the pastry bag and carefully spread the black over the already set white pieces to finish Pikachu's eyes. Repeat until you have 24 eyes in total.

9. For the ears, form the top black portion of the ears on the parchment paper. Repeat this until you have 24 of these shapes. Place yellow candy melts in a pastry bag. Heat up in the microwave for 30 seconds to 1 minute, until the candy melt is melted.

10. Cut the end of the pastry bag and shape the yellow part of Pikachu's ears on the prepared black tips. Repeat until you have 24 ear pieces.

11. Use the remaining melted black chocolate to shape Pikachu's mouth and nose. When placing these prepared candy melts on the tarts make sure to have the smooth bottom side face up.

To assemble Pikachu's face:

Create the eyes, mouth, nose, and ears with melted candy melts that have cooled and set. Place 2 raspberries for Pikachu's red cheeks.

Gengar
Yogurt Bowl

This yogurt bowl has a deep purple color like Gengar and is full of delicious nuts and fruit, making every spoonful smooth and complex. You may feel a sudden chill when working with the frozen fruit, but it's probably not a Gengar lurking in the shadows watching you cook.

Difficulty: ●●○○
Prep Time: 30 minutes
Rest Time: 45 minutes
Cook Time: 30 minutes
Yield: 1 to 2 bowls
Dietary Notes: Vegetarian

Equipment: Large bowl, spatula, small saucepan, 9-by-13-inch (23-by-33-centimeter) baking sheet, parchment paper, blender

Granola

3 cups (360 grams) old-fashioned rolled oats
½ cup (55 grams) walnuts, chopped
½ cup (55 grams) pecans, chopped
½ cup (112 grams) unsalted butter
⅓ cup (113 grams) honey
3 tablespoons (45 grams) brown sugar
½ teaspoon (2 grams) ground cardamom
½ teaspoon (2 grams) kosher salt
1 vanilla bean, seeds scraped and pod discarded
½ cup (70 grams) dried cherries
¼ cup (40 grams) dried blueberries

Berry Yogurt Mixture

1 cup (245 grams) plain yogurt
¾ cup (140 grams) frozen blueberries
½ cup (90 grams) frozen blackberries
1 banana

For assembly, per bowl

½ cups (75 grams) granola
Berry yogurt for serving
Shredded coconut flakes for garnishing
Fresh strawberries for garnishing

To make the granola:

1. Preheat oven to 350°F (177°C). Prepare a 9-by-13-inch baking sheet with a sheet of parchment paper. Combine the rolled oats, walnuts, and pecans in a large bowl. Set aside.

2. Combine the butter, honey, brown sugar, ground cardamom, salt, and vanilla bean seeds in a small saucepan. Place over medium heat and mix until the butter has melted and the sugar has dissolved. Carefully pour this into the large bowl with the oat mixture. Mix until well combined.

3. Transfer to the baking sheet and spread into a thin layer. Place in the oven and bake for 10 minutes. Stir and bake for another 10 minutes, or until golden brown. Remove from the oven and let cool for 45 minutes. Once cooled, transfer to an airtight container. Mix in the dried cherries and blueberries. This can be stored at room temperature in an airtight container for 10 days. This makes enough granola for about 10 portions.

To make the berry yogurt mixture:

Place the yogurt, frozen blueberries, frozen blackberries, and banana in a blender. Blend until smooth.

For assembly:

Place the granola at the bottom of a bowl. Add the berry yogurt. Top with coconut flakes, strawberries, and additional granola to your liking.

Seaking

Dragon Fruit Agua Fresca

Agua fresca is a delicious, refreshing drink that works all year round. But the perfect time to enjoy this drink is during autumn. Add the ice cubes and watch the drink turn a pretty shade of red.

Difficulty: ●○○○
Prep Time: 10 minutes
Rest Time: 8 hours
Yield: 4 to 6 servings
Dietary Notes: Vegan

Equipment: Blender, large pitcher, ice cube tray

Citrus Ice Cubes

2 grapefruits, juiced
1 blood orange, juiced
2 limes, juiced
½ cup (118 milliliters) water
2 tablespoons (30 milliliters) grenadine

Dragon Fruit Agua Fresca

3 dragon fruits (white flesh)
3 cups (710 milliliters) coconut water
¼ cup (52 grams) sugar
3 limes, juiced

To make the citrus ice cubes:

Combine all of the ingredients in a large cup. Transfer to a 12-slot ice cube tray. Place in the freezer for at least 8 hours before serving.

note: These ice cubes will be slightly softer than normal ice cubes.

To make the dragon fruit agua fresca:

1. Remove the skin of the dragon fruit. Cut the interior and transfer to a blender. Add the coconut water, sugar, and lime juice. Blend until smooth. Transfer to a large pitcher.

2. Taste and add additional lime juice if needed. Store in the refrigerator for 30 minutes to chill. The agua fresca can be stored for up to 3 days in the refrigerator.

3. To serve a portion, add 3 citrus ice cubes to a large glass. Shake the agua fresca if it has separated and pour into the prepared glass.

Dragonite
Butternut Squash Gnocchi

Kindhearted Dragonite simply must help people in need. After a bite of this gnocchi, you'll find yourself equally determined to help yourself to another serving of this delectable dish.

Difficulty: ●●○○
Prep Time: 30 minutes
Cook Time: 2 hours
Yield: 4 servings
Dietary Notes: Vegetarian

Equipment: Cutting board, knife, large baking sheet, blender, large pot, large nonstick pan

½ butternut squash, halved and seeded
1 tablespoon (15 milliliters) olive oil, plus more for greasing
Kosher salt
1 onion, chopped
4 garlic cloves, chopped
1 tablespoon (17 grams) shiro miso
½ teaspoon (2 grams) dried sage
13 ounces (384 milliliters) coconut milk
17 ounces (482 grams) premade gnocchi
¼ cup (56 grams) unsalted butter
10 fresh sage leaves, roughly chopped

1. Preheat oven to 375°F (191°C). Place the butternut squash (open side up) on a large baking sheet. Rub with olive oil and generously season with salt. Place in the oven and bake for 1 to 1½ hours, until the butternut squash is tender. Remove from the oven and allow to cool. Once cooled, carefully peel away the skin and place the flesh in a blender.
2. Place a large nonstick pan over medium-high heat. Add 1 tablespoon of olive oil and allow to heat up. Add the onion and cook until softened, about 5 minutes. Add the garlic and cook until softened, about 2 minutes. Remove from the heat and transfer to the blender.
3. Add the shiro miso, dried sage, and coconut milk to the blender. Blend until smooth. Set aside until the gnocchi is prepared.

note: The sauce should be relatively thick but not so thick that the blender can't blend all the ingredients together. If the mixture is too thick, add additional coconut milk.

4. Heat a large pot with water and salt over high heat. Bring to a boil and cook the gnocchi to the package's instructions. Reserve 2 cups (473 milliliters) of the water and drain the gnocchi.
5. Heat a large nonstick pan on medium-high heat. Add 2 tablespoons (28 grams) of butter and allow to melt. Add the gnocchi and panfry until they are golden brown, about 2 minutes per side. Transfer to 4 serving plates.
6. Add the remaining 2 tablespoons butter to the pan and let it melt. Add the fresh sage until it turns slightly brown, about 2 minutes. Transfer to another plate.
7. Add the blended butternut squash and cook until heated through. If the sauce becomes too thick, add a bit of the reserved water and mix in well. Top each of the plates of gnocchi with sauce and sprinkle with sage.

Johto Region

Furret

Ampharos

Shuckle

Umbreon

Swinub

Miltank

Furret

Fluffy Pancakes

Furret is super fluffy and able to squeeze into narrow spaces when it needs to get away. These pancakes are fluffy to match and have the same rings as Furret's tail. But if you eat too many, you won't be feeling as nimble as Furret.

Difficulty: ●●○○
Prep Time: 30 minutes
Rest Time: 20 minutes
Cook Time: 10 minutes per batch
Yield: 4 to 6 servings
Dietary Notes: Vegetarian

Equipment: Medium bowl, large bowl, whisk, medium nonstick pan

Vanilla Cardamom Pancakes

1 cup (141 grams) all-purpose flour
½ teaspoon (1 gram) ground cardamom
¼ teaspoon (½ gram) ground cinnamon
2 tablespoons (25 grams) sugar
½ vanilla bean, seeds scraped and pod discarded
1 teaspoon (4 grams) baking powder
½ teaspoon (2 grams) baking soda
1 pinch kosher salt
1 egg, separated
¾ cup (177 milliliters) buttermilk
2 tablespoons (28 grams) unsalted butter, melted and cooled
1 teaspoon (5 milliliters) vanilla extract
Nonstick cooking spray for greasing

Chocolate Pancakes

1 cup (141 grams) all-purpose flour
1 tablespoon (10 grams) cocoa powder
2 tablespoons (25 grams) sugar
1 teaspoon (4 grams) baking powder
½ teaspoon (2 grams) baking soda
1 pinch kosher salt
1 egg, separated
¾ cup (177 milliliters) buttermilk
2 tablespoons (28 grams) unsalted butter, melted and cooled
½ teaspoon (2½ milliliters) vanilla extract
Nonstick cooking spray for greasing
Black candy melts for decorating (optional)

Vanilla Cardamom Pancakes

1. Combine the flour, cardamom, cinnamon, sugar, vanilla bean seeds, baking powder, baking soda, and salt in a medium bowl. Place the egg white in a large bowl. Whisk until the egg white becomes frothy.

2. Add the egg yolk, buttermilk, melted butter, and vanilla extract to the egg white. Add the dry ingredients and fold in until it just comes together. Set aside and let rest for 20 minutes at room temperature.

3. Heat a medium nonstick pan over medium heat and spray with nonstick cooking spray. Take ¼ cup of the batter and place it on the pan. Allow the pancake to cook. The pancake is ready to flip once you begin to see small bubbles at the top, about 3 to 5 minutes. Flip the pancake and allow it to cook until the other side is golden brown, about another 2 minutes. Repeat with the remaining batter.

Chocolate Pancakes

1. Combine the flour, cocoa powder, sugar, baking powder, baking soda, and salt in a medium bowl. Place the egg white in a large bowl. Whisk until the egg white becomes frothy.

2. Add the egg yolk, buttermilk, melted butter, and vanilla extract to the egg white. Add the dry ingredients and fold in until it just comes together. Set aside and let rest for 20 minutes at room temperature.

3. Heat a medium nonstick pan over medium heat and spray with nonstick cooking spray. Take ¼ cup of the batter and place it on the pan. Allow the pancake to cook. The pancake is ready to flip once you begin to see small bubbles at the top, about 3 to 5 minutes. Flip the pancake and allow it to cook until the other side is golden brown, about another 2 minutes. Repeat with the remaining batter.

4. To serve, alternate the pancakes on a plate to match Furret's fur pattern. Make little eyes, cheek markings, and a mouth with candy melts. Place on the top pancake and enjoy.

note: Feel free to add whipped cream or syrup for dipping!

Ampharos
Lemonade

The light from Ampharos's tail is so bright that it can be seen from space! This lemonade isn't quite so bright, but it makes for a perfect thirst quencher.

Difficulty: ●○○○
Prep Time: 15 minutes
Rest Time: 8 hours
Cook Time: 10 minutes
Yield: 4 servings
Dietary Notes: Vegan

Equipment: Small saucepan, large pitcher, ice cube tray

Lemon Ice Cubes

3 lemons, juiced
2 lemons, zested

Simple Syrup

½ cup (118 milliliters) water
½ cup (110 grams) sugar
2 teaspoons (4 grams) citric acid
2 lemons, zested

Lemonade

¾ cup (177 milliliters) lemon juice (about 3 to 5 lemons)
2 to 3 cups (473 to 710 milliliters) water

To make the lemon ice cubes:

Combine all of the ingredients in a large cup. Transfer to a 12-slot ice cube tray. Place in the freezer for at least 8 hours before serving.

note: **These ice cubes will be slightly softer than normal ice cubes.**

To make the simple syrup:

Combine water, sugar, and citric acid in a small saucepan and place over medium-high heat. Whisk until the sugar has dissolved and bring to a boil. Reduce the heat and add the lemon zest. Simmer for 5 minutes. Remove the syrup from the heat and cool to room temperature.

To make the lemonade:

In a large pitcher, combine the simple syrup, lemon juice, and water. Mix together. Store in the refrigerator for at least 3 hours before serving. The lemonade can be stored in the refrigerator for up to 7 days.

Shuckle
Berry Juice

Shuckle likes to store berries in its shell where they eventually ferment into a delicious juice. Instead of waiting for a Shuckle, we can get our own berries and make juice just as delicious for ourselves.

Difficulty: ●○○○
Prep Time: 10 minutes
Yield: 2 drinks
Dietary Notes: Vegetarian

Equipment: Blender

1 (120 grams) banana
10 (125 grams) frozen strawberries
30 (75 grams) frozen raspberries
5 (8 grams) frozen blueberries
9 ounces (255 grams) frozen vanilla yogurt
¼ to ½ cup (59 to 118 milliliters) pomegranate juice

Place the banana and frozen berries in the blender. Blend until smooth. Add the frozen vanilla yogurt and ¼ cup of pomegranate juice and blend. If too thick, add more pomegranate juice.

Umbreon
Dark Chocolate Bagels

When Umbreon gets angry, it can secrete poison to ward off others. Although this bagel is perfectly fine to eat, it also has a strong bite that goes down great with some yellow sweetened cream cheese as a complement.

Difficulty: ●●●○
Prep Time: 1 hour
Rest Time: 12 hours
Cook Time: 25 minutes
Yield: 6 bagels
Dietary Notes: Vegetarian

Equipment: Small bowl, large bowl, large baking sheet, parchment paper, large pot

Sweetened Cream Cheese

8 ounces (225 grams) cream cheese, room temperature
4 drops yellow food dye (optional)
½ vanilla bean, seeds scraped and pod discarded
¼ cup (52 grams) sugar

Bagels

1 cup (237 milliliters) water, heated between 105° and 110°F (41° and 43°C)
1 tablespoon (22 grams) honey
2 ounces (57 grams) dark chocolate, melted
3 drops black food dye (optional)
2½ cups (385 grams) bread flour
2 tablespoons (17 grams) black cocoa powder
1 tablespoon (12 grams) vital wheat gluten
2 teaspoons (7 grams) active dry yeast
2 teaspoons (8 grams) kosher salt

Water Bath

8 cups (1,892 milliliters) water
¼ cup (66 grams) honey

Egg Wash

1 egg
1 tablespoon (15 milliliters) water

Sweetened Cream Cheese

Combine all the ingredients together until smooth. Cream cheese can be stored in an airtight container in the refrigerator for up to 2 weeks.

Bagels

1. Combine the water, honey, dark chocolate, and black food dye in a small bowl. Whisk until the honey is dissolved.
2. Combine bread flour, black cocoa powder, vital wheat gluten, yeast, and salt in a large bowl. Add the water mixture to the dry ingredients and mix until it just comes together. Once combined, let sit for 5 minutes.
3. Transfer to a countertop and knead for about 10 minutes. If the dough is still sticky, add additional flour. The end result will be a very firm dough. Place in an oiled bowl and cover. Let rest in the refrigerator overnight, at least 12 hours.
4. Remove the dough out of the refrigerator and split into 6 equal portions and form into balls. Cover with a kitchen towel and let rest for 20 minutes. Prepare a large baking sheet with parchment paper.
5. Take one of the dough balls and roll out flat until it is about 1 inch thick. Take one end and tightly roll the dough into a log.
6. Using your hands, roll the log until it is about 8 to 10 inches long. The ends should be slightly thinner than the center of the log.
7. Take the log and loop it around your hand. The ends should overlap with one another, about 2 to 3 inches. Pinch it together. With your hand in the center of the bagel, carefully roll the two ends together on the counter until they just come together.
8. Transfer to the baking sheet and repeat with the remaining dough portions. Cover and let rest for another 30 minutes. Preheat oven to 425°F (218°C).

To make the water bath

Combine the water and honey in a large pot. Bring to a boil. Place the bagels, but do not overcrowd, in the boiling water for 30 seconds per side and then place back on the baking sheet.

To make the egg wash

Whisk together the egg and water. Brush each bagel with the egg wash. Bake for 18 to 20 minutes, turning halfway through. Serve with the sweetened cream cheese.

Swinub

Truffles

Swinub may not look fast, but they'll go dashing at the first scent of something enticing. If you make these decadent truffles, be sure to hide them, or you may have a sudden swarm of Swinub on your hands!

Difficulty: ●●○○
Prep Time: 30 minutes
Rest Time: 4 hours
Cook Time: 5 minutes
Yield: 24 to 30 truffles
Dietary Notes: Vegetarian

Equipment: Cutting board, knife, medium bowl, medium saucepan, spatula, medium baking sheet, parchment paper, small bowl

14 ounces (340 grams) dark chocolate, chopped
2 tablespoons (28 grams) unsalted butter, room temperature
½ cup (118 milliliters) heavy cream
½ cup (155 grams) chocolate hazelnut spread
2 tablespoons (42 grams) honey
1 pinch kosher salt
3 tablespoons (15 grams) cocoa powder

1. Place 12 ounces chopped chocolate in a medium bowl. Place the butter and heavy cream in a medium saucepan and heat over low heat. Once the butter has melted and the cream is heated to just before a boil, pour over the chopped chocolate. Whisk together until smooth. If the chocolate does not completely melt, place in the microwave for 10 seconds at a time.

2. Mix in the chocolate hazelnut spread, honey, and salt. Allow to cool completely before placing in the refrigerator for 3 hours to solidify.

3. Prepare a baking sheet with parchment paper. Place the cocoa powder in a small bowl. Scoop out 1 tablespoon (24 grams) of the set chocolate. Roll between your hands to form a ball. Place in the bowl with the cocoa powder and toss to coat. Transfer to the prepared baking sheet. Repeat with the remaining chocolate.

note: If the chocolate becomes too warm to handle, place it back in the refrigerator for a couple of minutes to cool.

4. Place the remaining 2 ounces (56 grams) of dark chocolate in a pastry bag. Place in a microwave and heat until melted. Cut a small hole at the bottom and create the strips to match Swinub's fur pattern. Take your time with this because the chocolate might slip and slide off as you are placing it. Use a toothpick to help place the chocolate back on the truffle.

5. Once the truffles are all decorated, place the baking sheet in the refrigerator for 1 hour. Transfer the truffles to an airtight container and store in the refrigerator for up to 2 weeks.

Miltank

Milk Bread

Miltank's highly nutritious milk changes flavors with the season. Let's take some milk and make a fluffy milk bread with different flavors to match!

Difficulty: ●●○○
Prep Time: 30 minutes
Rest Time: 2 hours
Cook Time: 40 minutes
Yield: 2 loaves
Dietary Notes: Vegetarian

Equipment: Small saucepan, stand mixer with dough hook attachment, 2 large bowls, small bowl, 2 deep bread baking pans, aluminum foil

Egg wash

1 egg
2 tablespoons (30 milliliters) milk

Vanilla Dough

Tangzhong

2 tablespoons (20 grams) bread flour
⅓ cup (79 milliliters) milk

Dough

1 tablespoon (10 grams) active dry yeast
¾ cup (177 milliliters) warm milk
2¾ cups (430 grams) bread flour
1 teaspoon (4 grams) kosher salt
½ vanilla bean, seeds scraped and pod discarded
⅓ cup (80 grams) sugar
1 teaspoon (5 milliliters) vanilla extract
1 egg, room temperature
5 tablespoons (70 grams) unsalted butter, softened

Strawberry Dough

Tangzhong

2 tablespoons (25 grams) bread flour
⅓ cup (79 milliliters) milk

Dough

1 tablespoon (10 grams) active dry yeast
¼ cup (40 grams) strawberry powder
2 drops pink food dye (optional)
¾ cup (177 milliliters) warm milk
2¾ cups (430 grams) bread flour
1 teaspoon (4 grams) kosher salt
⅓ cup (70 grams) sugar
1 egg, room temperature
5 tablespoons (70 grams) unsalted butter, softened

Vanilla Dough

To make the tangzhong:

Place the bread flour and milk in a small saucepan over medium-high heat. Whisk until it comes together, about 1 minute. Set aside and allow to cool.

To make the dough:

1. Combine yeast and milk and let it rest for 5 minutes, allowing the yeast to become active.
2. Combine the bread flour, salt, vanilla bean seeds, and sugar in a large bowl of a stand mixer. Add the tangzhong, yeast mixture, vanilla extract, and egg to the bowl and mix until it just comes together.
3. While the dough begins to knead, add 1 tablespoon (14 grams) of butter at a time. Knead the dough for 5 minutes. If the dough is too sticky, add 1 tablespoon of flour at a time. If it is too dry, add 1 tablespoon of milk at a time.
4. Transfer to an oiled bowl, cover, and let rest for 1 hour, or until it has doubled in size.

Strawberry Dough

To make the tangzhong:

Place the bread flour and milk in a small saucepan over medium-high heat. Whisk until it comes together, about 1 minute. Set aside and allow to cool.

To make the dough:

1. Combine yeast, strawberry powder, pink food dye, and milk and let it rest for 5 minutes, allowing the yeast to become active.
2. Combine the bread flour, salt, and sugar in a large bowl of a stand mixer. Add the tangzhong, yeast mixture, and egg to the bowl and mix until it just comes together.
3. While the dough begins to knead, add the butter 1 tablespoon (14 grams) at a time. Knead the dough for 5 minutes. If the dough is too sticky, add 1 tablespoon of flour at a time. If it is too dry, add 1 tablespoon of milk at a time.
4. Transfer to an oiled bowl, cover, and let rest for 1 hour, or until it has doubled in size.

continued on the next page

For assembly and baking:

1. Once both doughs have doubled, punch down and knead. Split each dough into 3 equal portions. You will have 3 vanilla dough balls and 3 strawberry dough balls. Grease 2 deep bread baking pans.

2. For the first loaf, take one of the strawberry portions and roll the dough out into a long rectangle. Make sure the width of the rolled-out portion is not wider than the baking pan you are using. Carefully roll up the dough. Place in one of the prepared baking pans. Take a vanilla portion and repeat the process. Place the vanilla portion next to the strawberry. Take another strawberry portion, repeat the process, and place next to the vanilla portion.

3. Repeat step 2 for the second loaf.

note: The first loaf will be 2 parts strawberry and 1 part vanilla, while the second loaf will be 2 parts vanilla and 1 part strawberry. I like to alternate the 2 flavors to make a colorful loaf.

4. Cover and allow to rise again for 45 minutes, or until it doubles in size. Preheat oven to 350°F (177°C).

5. In a small bowl, combine the egg and milk for the egg wash. Brush the top of the loaves with the egg wash. Place in the oven and bake for 15 minutes. Lightly cover each of the loaves with aluminum foil to avoid browning too much. Cook for another 15 to 25 minutes, until cooked through.

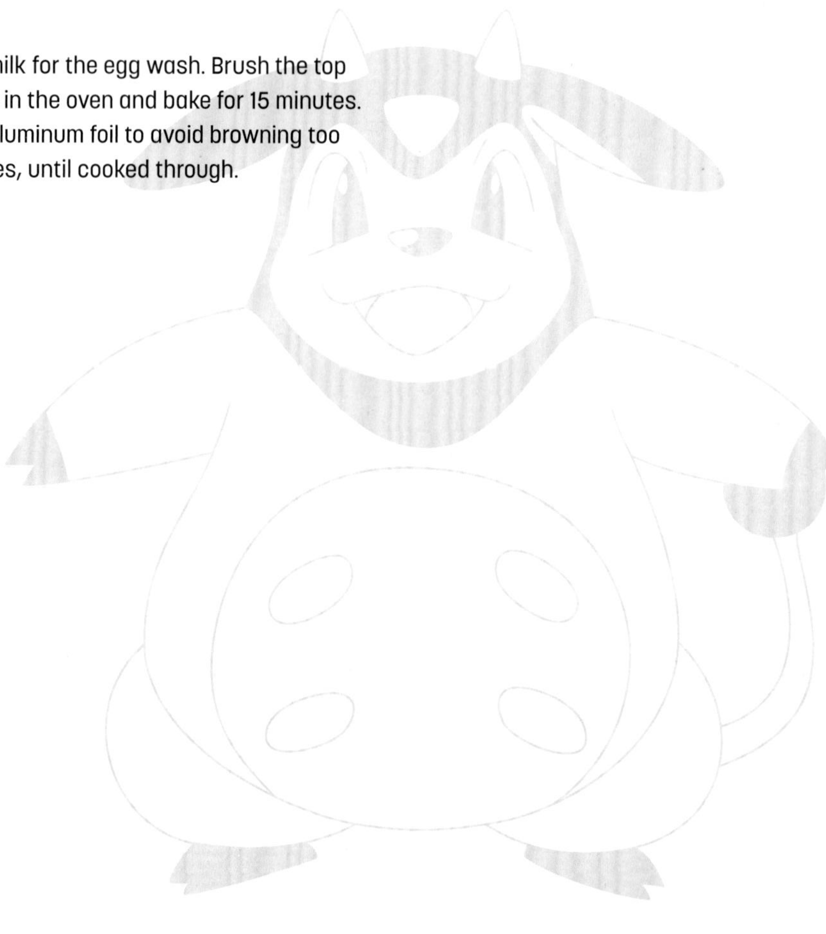

Hoenn Region

Marshtomp

Breloom

Swalot

Spinda

Flygon

Relicanth

Marshtomp

Umeboshi Onigiri

Marshtomp loves playing in the mud on beaches during low tide. Try to mold these onigiri after Marshtomp, capturing the joy it has for getting muddy and sliding around!

Difficulty: ●●●○
Prep Time: 40 minutes
Cook Time: 45 minutes
Yield: 10 onigiri
Dietary Notes: Vegan

Equipment: Rice cooker, fine mesh strainer (optional), medium nonmetallic bowl, small bowl

Blue Sushi Rice

3 cups (424 grams) sushi rice
12 butterfly pea flowers (or blue food coloring)
Water (follow your rice cooker's directions)
2 tablespoons (30 milliliters) rice vinegar
1 tablespoon (15 grams) sugar
½ teaspoon (2 grams) kosher salt

For Assembly

10 orange umeboshi, halved
1 small carrot, peeled
Black sesame seeds for decorating
Pickled ginger for decorating
Nori sheets for decorating

To make the blue sushi rice:

1. Place rice in a bowl and cover with cold water. With your hands, rub in a circular motion. The water will become opaque. Strain the water out and repeat until the water is clear.

note: You can use a fine mesh strainer to help you with the draining process to avoid losing any rice grains. One option is to put the rice in the mesh strainer and place it in the bowl. Fill with water, rub, remove the strainer from the bowl, pour out the water, and repeat.

2. Place the cleaned rice, butterfly pea flowers, and amount of water required into a rice cooker and allow the rice to cook. When the rice is done, remove from the rice cooker and place inside a medium nonmetallic bowl. Remove the butterfly pea flowers.

3. Combine rice vinegar, sugar, and salt in a small bowl. Add the vinegar mixture to the rice while the rice is still hot. Take a rice paddle and fold in the rice vinegar. Continue to fold and slice the rice until it has cooled down.

note: You can also add a drop or two of light blue food dye to the vinegar mixture in order to have the color pop more. It's a good idea to wait until the rice is done cooking to make that decision.

To assemble the onigiri:

1. Have a small bowl of water to keep your hands moist during the process. Wet your hands and then take a handful of the rice mixture and begin forming large oval shapes. Use a moderate amount of pressure to make sure they are formed correctly.

2. Take 2 umeboshi halves and place them on the sides for Marshtomp's cheeks. Place 1 small, julienned carrot slice in the center of each umeboshi and pierce through to the rice.

3. To shape the eyes, take 2 small carrot slices and shape into an oval shape matching Marshtomp's eye shape. Carefully take a black sesame seed and wet it. Place in the center of the carrot.

4. Take a piece of pickled ginger to shape the mouth. Take a second piece and cut it to make the tongue. Finally, top with a piece of nori to match the top fin.

Breloom

Spring Rolls

If you want to put a spring to your step just like Breloom, why not enjoy some spring rolls? They are light and flavorful, and will keep you feeling refreshed and ready for whatever activities you have planned.

Difficulty: ●●●○
Prep Time: 1 hour
Cook Time: 30 minutes
Yield: 14 spring rolls
Dietary Notes: Vegan

Equipment: Cutting board, knife, large bowl, large nonstick pan

Spring Rolls

16 ounces (375 grams) firm tofu
Salt
Pepper
¼ cup (38 grams) cornstarch
1 teaspoon (5 milliliters) canola oil
Lukewarm water
14 round rice paper sheets
1 head butter lettuce
8 ounces (227 grams) rice vermicelli, cooked and cooled
1 cucumber, peeled and cut into long, thin slices
2 carrots, peeled and julienned
1 red bell pepper, thinly sliced
10 radishes, thinly sliced
⅓ cup (50 grams) fresh cilantro
⅓ cup (45 grams) fresh mint
3 ounces (85 grams) fresh Thai basil

Peanut Sauce

¼ cup (90 grams) smooth peanut butter
3 garlic cloves, minced
1 tablespoon (15 milliliters) rice vinegar
1 tablespoon (15 milliliters) soy sauce
3 tablespoons (45 milliliters) coconut milk
1 lime, juiced
1 tablespoon (20 grams) maple syrup
1 teaspoon (5 milliliters) sesame oil

To make the spring rolls:

1. Place the tofu between two plates and top with a heavy object. Allow to rest for 5 minutes to remove excess liquid. Cut the tofu into 14 rectangle pieces. Season with salt and pepper. Toss in cornstarch, covering all sides, and set aside.
2. Heat a large nonstick large nonstick pan with canola oil over medium-high heat. Add the tofu and cook until all sides have slightly browned, about 3 minutes per side. Transfer to a plate.
3. Fill a deep dish, large enough to fit a piece of rice paper, with lukewarm water. Soak a rice paper sheet in the dish until it softens slightly. Place on a cutting board.
4. Place a piece of butter lettuce in the lower half of the rice paper sheet.
5. Add a portion of vermicelli, 1 piece of tofu, 2 to 3 slices of cucumber, a small portion of carrots, 1 to 2 slices of red bell pepper, several pieces of radish, and the herbs on top of the butter lettuce.
6. Grab the lower edge of the rice paper and start rolling the lettuce portion. When you just begin to cover all the fillings, about halfway up, tuck the sides inward. Continuing rolling until sealed.

note: The rice paper will get softer and softer as it sits out. Do these one at a time to make sure the rice paper isn't too difficult to wrap up.

To make the peanut sauce:

Combine all the ingredients in a bowl. Serve immediately or store in the refrigerator until you are ready to serve.

Swalot

Ube Flan

Though it may be tempting to imitate Swalot's eating habits and swallow this entire ube flan in one gulp, habits like that are only good for Swalot. You'll enjoy this treat if you take your time and savor every bite.

Difficulty: ●●○○
Prep Time: 30 minutes
Rest Time: 4 hours
Cook Time: 1 hour
Yield: 6 servings
Dietary Notes: Vegetarian

Equipment: Medium saucepan, six 3½-inch (9-centimeter) ramekins, large deep baking dish, medium bowl, large bowl, parchment paper, large baking sheet

Chocolate Sugar Cookie

1½ cups (240 grams) all-purpose flour
1 tablespoon (8 grams) black cocoa powder
½ teaspoon (2 grams) kosher salt
½ cup (112 grams) unsalted butter, room temperature
½ cup (110 grams) sugar
1 egg
2 teaspoons (10 milliliters) vanilla extract

Flan

⅔ cup (150 grams) sugar
¼ cup (59 milliliters) water
1 teaspoon (5 grams) kosher salt
3 eggs
2 egg yolks
14 ounces (198 grams) sweetened condensed milk
12 ounces (170 grams) evaporated milk
2 teaspoons (10 milliliters) ube extract
1 tablespoon (15 milliliters) vanilla extract

To make the chocolate sugar cookie:

1. Combine all-purpose flour, black cocoa powder, and salt in a medium bowl. Cream the butter in a large bowl. Add the sugar and mix until combined and slightly fluffy. Add the egg and vanilla extract. Finally, add the flour mixture and whisk together until it is just combined.

2. Place the dough on a sheet of parchment paper. Lightly flour the portion and then cover with another sheet of parchment paper. Roll the dough out to ¼ to ½ inch (6 to 13 millimeters) thickness. Cover and place in the refrigerator and let rest for at least 1 hour.

3. Preheat oven to 350°F (177°C). After the dough has rested, take it out and place it on a floured surface. Carefully cut out the cookies with a cookie cutter. Place the cutout cookies on a large baking sheet covered in parchment paper. Reshape the remaining dough and roll it out once again. Cut out more cookies. Repeat this until you have used up all the dough. Bake for 8 to 10 minutes, or until the center is set and firm.

note: This will make many more cookies than you would need to set up the ube flan.

To make the flan:

1. Preheat oven to 350°F (177°C). Combine sugar and water in a medium saucepan over medium-low heat. Allow to simmer for 15 minutes, until it turns golden. Immediately add the salt and stir in. Pour the caramel from the saucepan into six 3½-inch (9-centimeter) ramekins. Rotate the ramekins around to spread it evenly on the bottom.

2. Combine the whole eggs, egg yolks, sweetened condensed milk, evaporated milk, ube extract, and vanilla extract in a medium bowl until smooth. Pour the mixture in the ramekins.

3. Place the ramekins inside a large deep baking dish. Fill the baking dish around the ramekins with water about halfway up the ramekins. Place in the oven and bake for 40 to 50 minutes, or until the internal temp reaches 175°F (79°C).

4. Remove the ramekins from the baking dish and allow them to cool. Once they are completely cooled, place in a refrigerator for at least 3 hours before serving. To remove them from the ramekins, run a knife along the side, place a plate upside down over the ramekin, and flip upright. Serve with the chocolate sugar cookies.

Spinda

Raspberry Marble Cake

Every Spinda's spot pattern is different. These marble cakes are made with beautiful swirls, so try to make a unique swirl pattern with each!

Difficulty: ●●○○
Prep Time: 45 minutes
Cook Time: 20 to 25 minutes
Yield: 8 mini cakes
Dietary Notes: Vegetarian

Equipment: Blender, fine mesh strainer, stand mixer with paddle, medium bowl, 8-cavity mini loaf pan, wire rack

4 ounces (113 grams) fresh raspberries
2 drops red food dye
1 drop orange food dye
2 cups (290 grams) cake flour
2 teaspoons (9 grams) baking powder
1 teaspoon (4 grams) kosher salt
⅔ cup (151 grams) unsalted butter, room temperature
1 cup (225 grams) sugar
4 egg whites, room temperature
1 teaspoon (5 milliliters) vanilla extract
⅔ cup (158 milliliters) buttermilk, room temperature

1. Preheat oven to 350°F (177°C). Place the raspberries in a blender and purée them. Pour the puréed raspberries through a fine mesh strainer to remove the seeds. Mix in the food dye and set aside.
2. Combine the cake flour, baking powder, and salt in a medium bowl. Set aside. Place the butter in the bowl of a stand mixer and cream until fluffy. Add the sugar and mix until smooth. Add the egg whites and vanilla extract. Mix until combined.
3. Add half of the dry ingredients into the stand mixer and mix. Add the buttermilk and mix until smooth. Add the remaining dry ingredients and mix until just combined.
4. Pour half of the mixture into another bowl. To that bowl, add the puréed raspberries and mix until the color of the batter is uniform.
5. Prepare the 8-cavity mini loaf pan by spraying with nonstick oil. Spoon in each of the batters, alternating to create unique patterns.

note: Make sure you can see some of the vanilla and raspberry batter at the top. Have fun with this and make your own combinations.

6. Place in the oven and bake for 18 to 25 minutes, or until a toothpick test comes out clean. Allow to rest for 5 minutes and then remove from the pan onto a wire rack.

Flygon

Avocado Toast

Spotting a Flygon is a rare occurrence. It would rather hide in the hearts of sandstorms than fly around in public. Try to see if you can remember what Flygon looks like by making your own Flygon on a piece of delicious avocado toast. Don't be as elusive, show off your best avocado toast Flygon to your friends and family!

Difficulty: ●○○○
Prep Time: 30 minutes
Yield: 4 servings
Dietary Notes: Vegetarian

Equipment: Medium bowl, cutting board, knife

4 ounces (113 grams) cream cheese, room temperature
1 ounce (28 grams) sour cream
½ tablespoon (7 milliliters) lemon juice
1 teaspoon (2 grams) lemon zest
¼ teaspoon (1 gram) kosher salt
¼ teaspoon (½ gram) black pepper
1 teaspoon (1 gram) dill leaves
4 slices thick white bread
2 avocados, sliced
1 tomato, sliced
3 scallions, dark green part only
Pomegranate arils for garnishing

1. Whisk together the cream cheese and sour cream in a medium bowl. Add lemon juice, lemon zest, salt, black pepper, and dill leaves. Mix until just combined. Place in an airtight container. The cream cheese mixture can be stored in the refrigerator for up to 1 week.

2. Toast the white bread to your liking. Place each of the pieces of toast on a plate and cover with the cream cheese mixture. Top with avocado, tomato, scallions, and pomegranate arils.

note: **You can use all of these elements to shape the toppings to look just like Flygon.**

Relicanth

Chocolate Malt

This chocolate malt has an intense, deep flavor, inspired by Relicanth's natural deep-sea habitat. It's dark and murky but oh so delicious. Don't forget the cherry to match Relicanth's marking!

Difficulty: ●○○○
Prep Time: 30 minutes
Yield: 2 malts
Dietary Notes: Vegetarian

Equipment: Stand mixer with whisk attachment, blender

Chocolate Whipped Cream

½ cup (118 milliliters) heavy cream
2 tablespoons (14 grams) cocoa powder
1 tablespoon (10 grams) powdered sugar

Dark Chocolate Malt Layer

1 tablespoon (12 grams) black cocoa powder
3 tablespoons (30 grams) malted milk powder
2 ounces (59 milliliters) whole milk
11 ounces (310 grams) chocolate ice cream
2 maraschino cherries

To make the chocolate whipped cream:

Place all the ingredients into a bowl of a stand mixer. Mix on medium-high speed until the whipped cream forms stiff peaks, about 3 to 5 minutes. Transfer to a piping bag and store in the refrigerator until needed.

To make the dark chocolate malt layer:

1. In a blender, add the black cocoa powder, malted milk powder, and milk. Blend until combined. Add the ice cream and blend until smooth. If the mixture is too thick, add a small amount of milk.

2. Pour about halfway up in two large glasses. Take the prepared whipped cream and add a layer of it on top. Add the remaining chocolate malt on top. Top each with additional whipped cream and a maraschino cherry.

Sinnoh Region

Combee

Drifloon

Munchlax

Abomasnow

Weavile

Frosslass

Combee
Honey Cookies

Combee are a trio, working together all day to gather nectar. When you frost these cookies, you can make all sorts of Combee faces and combine them for silly groupings.

Difficulty: ●●○○
Prep Time: 30 minutes
Rest Time: 1 hour
Cook Time: 15 minutes
Yield: 24 cookies
Dietary Notes: Vegetarian

Equipment: Medium bowl, large bowl, 2 large baking sheets, parchment paper, hexagon cookie cutter

3¾ cups (562 grams) all-purpose flour
1 teaspoon (3 grams) ground ginger
1 teaspoon (4 grams) kosher salt
1 cup (224 grams) unsalted butter, room temperature
½ cup (114 grams) sugar
½ cup (170 grams) honey
2 eggs
1 teaspoon (5 milliliters) vanilla extract
Black candy melts for decorating

1. Combine the flour, ginger, and salt in a medium bowl. Cream the butter in a large bowl. Add the sugar and honey. Mix until combined and slightly fluffy. Add the eggs and vanilla extract. Finally, add the flour mixture and whisk together until it is just combined. Split the dough in half.

2. Take one of the halves and transfer onto a sheet of parchment paper. Lightly flour the portion and then cover with another sheet of parchment paper. Roll the dough out to ¼ to ½ inch thickness. Cover and place in the refrigerator to rest for at least 1 hour. Repeat this step with the other half of the dough.

3. Preheat oven to 350°F (177°C). After the dough has rested, take one of the doughs out and place it on a very floured surface. Carefully use a cookie cutter to cut out the cookies. Place the cutout cookies on a large baking sheet covered with parchment paper. Reshape the remaining dough and roll it out once again. Cut out more cookies. Repeat this until you have used up all the dough. Bake for 12 to 15 minutes, or until golden brown.

4. Allow the cookies to completely cool before icing them. Use black candy melts to add Combee faces.

Drifloon

Blackberry Marshmallows

These marshmallows are so fluffy and violet, you'd think they would float away just like Drifloon. You could even cut them out in fun Drifloon shapes if you'd like.

Difficulty: ●●○○
Prep Time: 30 minutes
Rest Time: 24 hours
Cook Time: 15 minutes
Yield: 24 large marshmallows

Equipment: Food processor, fine mesh strainer, medium saucepan, candy thermometer, stand mixer with whisk attachment, 9-by-13-inch (23-by-33-centimeter) deep baking pan

8 ounces (227 grams) fresh blackberries
Cold water
2½ tablespoons (20 grams) unflavored gelatin
3 drops purple food dye (optional)
1¾ cups (360 grams) sugar
½ cup (165 grams) light corn syrup
½ teaspoon (2 grams) kosher salt
1 teaspoon (5 milliliters) vanilla extract
Nonstick cooking spray for greasing
Confectioners' sugar for dusting
Yellow candy melts for decorating
Whipped cream for decorating

1. Place the blackberries in a food processor and blend until smooth. Transfer to a measuring cup by passing the liquid through a fine mesh strainer to remove any seeds. Add cold water to the measuring cup to have the liquid equal 1 cup (237 milliliters) in total.

2. Pour half of the blackberry mixture into a stand mixer. Add the gelatin and purple food dye. Whisk everything together and set aside.

3. Over medium-high heat, combine the remaining half of the blackberry mixture, sugar, corn syrup, and salt in a medium saucepan. Stir together. Cook until the mixture reaches 240°F (116°C). Remove from the heat.

4. Set the stand mixer to slow. Slowly pour the sugar mixture into the stand mixer while running. Turn the mixer to high and mix for 10 to 15 minutes, or until it thickens. Near the end, add the vanilla extract.

note: If you notice the mixture has lightened too much, feel free to add additional purple food dye.

5. Prepare the baking pan by spraying with nonstick cooking spray and sprinkling with confectioners' sugar.

6. Transfer the sugar mixture into the pan and spread evenly. Sprinkle the top with confectioners' sugar. Allow the marshmallows to rest, uncovered, overnight. Use an oiled knife to cut the marshmallows to your desired size. The marshmallows can be stored in an airtight container for up to 2 weeks.

7. To serve, use yellow candy melts to shape an X matching Drifloon's marking. Serve each marshmallow portion with an X and a bit of whipped cream.

Munchlax

Custard Bao

All Munchlax thinks about is eating a vast amount of food. I bet it could even eat all 10 bao from this recipe! But be careful! You'll have a serious stomachache if you try the same. It would be best to share them or save some for later!

Difficulty: ●●●●
Prep Time: 3 hours
Rest Time: 12 hours
Cook Time: 45 minutes
Yield: 10 bao
Dietary Notes: Vegetarian

Equipment: 2 large bowls, small bowl, whisk, fine mesh strainer, medium saucepan, stand mixer with dough hook attachment, rolling pin, parchment paper, large pot with steamer basket

Custard Filling

4 egg yolks
½ vanilla bean, seeds scraped and pod discarded
½ cup (119 grams) sugar
1¾ cups (414 milliliters) whole milk
5 tablespoons (48 grams) all-purpose flour
2 tablespoons (20 grams) cornstarch
½ teaspoon (2 grams) kosher salt
¼ cup (56 grams) unsalted butter, melted and cooled
1 teaspoon (2½ milliliters) vanilla extract

White Dough

2 teaspoons (8 grams) active dry yeast
1 cup (237 milliliters) warm whole milk
2½ cups (385 grams) all-purpose flour
½ cup (74 grams) cornstarch
1½ teaspoons (6 grams) baking powder
¼ cup (55 grams) sugar
2 teaspoons (8 grams) kosher salt
2 tablespoons (28 grams) unsalted butter, room temperature

Blue Dough

½ teaspoon (2 grams) active dry yeast
¼ cup (59 milliliters) warm whole milk
½ cup plus 2 tablespoons (96 grams) all-purpose flour
2 tablespoons (18 grams) cornstarch
⅓ teaspoon (2 grams) baking powder
1 tablespoon (14 grams) sugar
½ teaspoon (2 grams) kosher salt
½ tablespoon (7 grams) unsalted butter, room temperature
Blue and black food dye for coloring

note: It is very important that the milk is no warmer than 110°F (43°C) because if it is any warmer, it will kill the yeast and not allow the dough to rise. You can use a meat thermometer to check the temperature.

To make the custard filling:

1. Combine the egg yolks, vanilla bean seeds, and sugar in a large bowl. Whisk together until completely combined. Add the milk and whisk until well combined. Combine the flour, cornstarch, and salt in a small bowl. Add the butter and flour mixture to the bowl with the egg yolks. Whisk together until well combined.

2. Place a fine mesh strainer over a medium saucepan. Pass the mixture through the mesh strainer. Make sure to press everything through if it has clumped up. Whisk the mixture in the saucepan over medium heat until the mixture thickens into a thick paste, about 15 to 25 minutes. Once thickened, remove from the heat and whisk in the vanilla extract.

3. Transfer to an airtight container and allow to cool completely. Place a piece of plastic wrap directly over it, cover, and allow to rest in the refrigerator overnight, or at least 12 hours.

4. After it has rested, split the thickened custard into 10 portions. Take each portion and roll into a ball in your hands. Return to the container, cover, and place back into the refrigerator until needed.

To make the white dough:

1. Combine the yeast and milk. Allow to rest for 5 minutes, or until the yeast becomes active. Combine the flour, cornstarch, baking powder, sugar, and salt in a bowl of a stand mixer. Slowly mix in the liquid with the flour at a low speed. Mix until it all comes together.

2. Increase the speed to medium and allow to lightly knead. While the dough begins to knead, add the butter slowly. Knead the dough for 5 minutes. If the dough is too sticky, add 1 tablespoon of flour at a time. If it is too dry, add 1 tablespoon of milk at a time. Transfer to an oiled bowl, cover, and let rest for 2 hours, or until it has doubled in size.

continued on the next page

To make the blue dough:

Repeat steps 1 and 2 of the white dough directions with one minor difference. Add the blue food dye to the yeast and milk mixture. You may need several drops for a vibrant color, depending on the strength of your food dye.

To combine and bake:

1. Punch down the white dough and roll out to remove the air pockets. Set aside about 2 tablespoons of dough for the eyes and teeth. Split into 10 equal portions. Take each portion and form into a smooth ball. Cover with a kitchen towel and let rest for 15 minutes.

2. Take a portion and roll out to about 5 inches wide. When rolling, make sure the center is thicker than the edges. Add one of the custard portions in the center. Wet your finger and lightly wet the edge of the dough. Pleat the buns until sealed. Flip the pleat side down and gently roll with your hand to smooth it out slightly. Place on a piece of parchment paper, pleat side down. Repeat with the remaining portions.

3. Take a fourth of the set-aside white dough and add a drop of black food dye. Rub together until it is dyed black. This will be used for the pupils.

> **note:** You can use disposable, food safe gloves to avoid dying your hands.

4. Take the blue dough and roll it out very thin. Cut into a circle and cut the bottom fifth of the dough off. Take one of the baos. Lightly wet the prepared blue dough and drape over the bao. Wrap it and press into the bottom to stick to the dough.

5. Take 1 tablespoon of the blue dough and shape into one of Munchlax's ears.

6. Lightly wet the bottom and attach it to the top of the bao. Repeat this step for the other ear.

7. Take a small portion of the set-aside white dough and shape into 2 eyes and 2 teeth. Wet and place them on the bao to mimic Munchlax's face. Take a small amount of the black and make it into pupils. Place the completed Munchlax bao in a steamer basket.

8. Repeat steps 7–9 with the remaining portions.

9. Let the prepared bao rest for 30 minutes. Heat a pot that the steamer basket can sit on with water over high heat and bring to a boil. Once boiling, reduce the heat to medium and place the steamer basket on top. Allow to steam for 15 to 20 minutes, until cooked through.

10. Turn off the heat and let sit, covered, for 5 minutes before serving the buns. This will help to prevent them from shrinking.

Abomasnow
Vichyssoise

Abomasnow has a massive body covered in snow and can cause blizzards on its own. Luckily, a nearby Abomasnow causing a blizzard won't ruin our vichyssoise. It's a soup that's served cold!

Difficulty: ●●○○
Prep Time: 30 minutes
Rest Time: 12 hours
Cook Time: 30 minutes
Yield: 4 to 6 servings
Dietary Notes: Vegan

Equipment: Large pot, blender, fine mesh strainer

2 tablespoons (30 milliliters) coconut oil
10 ounces (283 grams) leeks
1½ pounds (680 grams) Yukon gold potatoes, peeled and quartered
4 cups (946 milliliters) vegetable broth
1 bay leaf
½ cup (118 milliliters) coconut cream
Kosher salt
White ground pepper
Fresh chives, finely chopped, for garnishing

1. Place a large pot with coconut oil over medium-high heat. Allow the coconut oil to melt and add the leeks. Cook until the leeks are completely softened, about 8 minutes.

2. Add the potatoes and toss to mix. Add the vegetable broth and bay leaf. Bring to a boil. Reduce to medium-low and simmer until the potatoes are tender, about 30 minutes.

3. Remove the bay leaf. Transfer everything else to a blender and blend until smooth. Pour through a fine mesh strainer into an airtight container. Add the coconut cream and mix together. Season with salt and pepper to your liking. Allow to cool completely, cover, and place in the refrigerator for at least 1 hour before serving. Serve in a bowl with chopped chives on top.

Weavile
Ice Pops

Just like how Weavile works in a team, you'll want some friends to finish all these ice pops. Otherwise, you'll get brain freeze!

Difficulty: ●○○○
Prep Time: 30 minutes
Rest Time: 12 hours
Yield: 6 ice pops
Dietary Notes: Vegan, gluten-free

Equipment: Blender, ice pop molds

Raspberry Layer

3½ ounces (99 grams) frozen raspberries
¾ cup (177 milliliters) coconut milk
1 tablespoon (16 grams) sugar
½ teaspoon (2½ milliliters) vanilla extract

Black Sesame Layer

⅓ cup (45 grams) black sesame seeds
½ cup (88 grams) chopped dark chocolate
1 cup (237 milliliters) coconut milk
¼ cup (60 grams) sugar
½ teaspoon (2½ milliliters) almond extract
½ teaspoon (2 grams) kosher salt

To make the raspberry layer:

1. Place all the ingredients in a blender and blend until smooth.

2. Transfer the mixture into ice pop molds and fill each a third of the way up. Place in the freezer (without the sticks) for 30 minutes.

To make the black sesame layer:

1. Place the sesame seeds in a blender and blend until smooth. Scrape the side of the blender a few times while blending to make sure most of the seeds are blended.

2. Add the dark chocolate, coconut milk, sugar, almond extract, and salt. Blend until completely smooth and well combined.

3. Transfer the mixture into your ice pop molds on top of the raspberry layer. Place the ice pop sticks in, cover, and place in the freezer overnight, at least 12 hours.

Froslass

Blackberry Ice Cream

Froslass loves frozen food, but we won't be adding any of that to this frozen dessert. Berries will do nicely to add some great flavor and a beautiful swirl.

Difficulty: ●●○○
Prep Time: 30 minutes
Rest Time: 12 hours
Cook Time: 30 minutes
Yield: 6 to 8 servings
Dietary Notes: Vegetarian

Equipment: Medium saucepan, fine mesh strainer, large bowl, stand mixer with whisk attachment

Blackberry Sauce

14 ounces (396 grams) fresh blackberries
2 tablespoons (30 grams) sugar
1 teaspoon (4 grams) kosher salt
1 lemon, zested and juiced

Vanilla Ice Cream

14 ounces (396 grams) sweetened condensed milk
1 vanilla bean, seeds scraped and pod discarded
1 tablespoon (5 milliliters) vanilla extract
1 pinch kosher salt
2 cups (473 milliliters) heavy cream
Blackberry sauce

To make the blackberry sauce:

1. Combine all the ingredients in a medium saucepan. Place over medium-high and bring to a boil. Smash the blackberries. Reduce the heat and simmer for 20 minutes.

2. Remove from the heat and strain through a fine mesh strainer into an airtight container. Once cooled, cover and store in the refrigerator for at least 12 hours and up to 2 weeks.

note: You can skip the step of straining through a fine mesh strainer if you would like chunks of the fruit left in the ice cream. Either way will be delicious.

To make the vanilla ice cream:

1. Combine the sweetened condensed milk, vanilla bean seeds, vanilla extract, and salt in a large bowl. Whisk together until well combined.

2. Place the heavy cream into a bowl of a stand mixer. Mix until the whipped cream forms medium peaks, abut 2 to 3 minutes. Transfer to the bowl with everything else. Carefully fold in the whipped cream until it is well combined.

3. Transfer to an airtight container, placing a third of the vanilla ice cream mixture in it. Pour half of the blackberry sauce and swirl it slightly into the vanilla mixture. Add another third of the vanilla mixture. Add the remaining blackberry sauce and top with the remaining vanilla mixture. Swirl slightly once more. Cover and place in the freezer for at least 5 hours before serving.

Unova Region

Pansage, Pansear, and Panpour

Masharna

Swadloon

Darumaka

Crustle

Stunfisk

Pansear, Pansage, and Panpour

Roasted Cauliflower

Pansear, Pansage, and Panpour have their own strengths and weaknesses, but they love to be helpful to others. Why not help yourself to some tasty dips inspired by their unique attitudes?

Difficulty: ●○○○
Prep Time: 45 minutes
Cook Time: 20 minutes
Yield: 4 servings
Dietary Notes: Vegetarian

Equipment: Large bowl, large baking sheet, aluminum foil, airtight containers, food processor

Roasted Cauliflower

2 cauliflowers, cut into large portions
¼ cup (59 milliliters) olive oil
1 teaspoon (4 grams) garlic powder
Nonstick cooking spray for greasing
Kosher salt
Ground black pepper

Buffalo Sauce

¼ cup (59 milliliters) hot sauce
1 tablespoon (24 grams) gochujang
½ tablespoon (10 grams) maple syrup
¼ cup (56 grams) unsalted butter, melted
1 tablespoon (15 milliliters) rice vinegar
½ teaspoon (2 grams) cayenne pepper

Blue Cheese Dipping Sauce

3 ounces (85 grams) blue cheese, crumbled
¼ cup (55 grams) mayonnaise
3 tablespoons (45 grams) sour cream
3 tablespoons (45 milliliters) buttermilk
½ tablespoon (8 milliliters) lemon juice
1 drop of light blue food dye
Kosher salt
Ground black pepper

Green Chutney

½ bunch fresh cilantro
1 serrano chile, stemmed
3 garlic cloves
One ½-inch (12-millimeter) piece fresh ginger
1 teaspoon (4 grams) sugar
½ teaspoon (2 grams) kosher salt
1 lime, juiced
1½ tablespoons (22 milliliters) water
1 tablespoon (12 milliliters) yogurt

To make the roasted cauliflower:

1. Preheat oven to 425°F (218°C). Place the cauliflower portions, olive oil, and garlic powder in a large bowl. Toss until combined.

2. Prepare a large baking sheet with aluminum foil and spray with nonstick cooking spray. Transfer the cauliflower to the prepared baking sheet. Season generously with salt and pepper.

3. Place in the oven and bake for 15 minutes. Toss and bake for another 10 minutes, until golden and tender.

To make the buffalo sauce:

Combine all the ingredients. The buffalo sauce can be stored in an airtight container for up to 1 week.

To make the green chutney:

Place all the ingredients in a food processor and pulse until smooth. If the mixture is too thick, add a small amount of water at a time to loosen it. The chutney can be stored in an airtight container in the refrigerator for up to 1 week.

To make the blue cheese dipping sauce:

Combine all the ingredients. Season with salt and pepper. The dipping sauce can be stored in an airtight container for up to 1 week.

Musharna

Strawberry Taro Slush

This strawberry and taro slush has its own beautiful pink swirls, reminiscent of the dark mist that emanates from a Musharna. It's sure to bring joy to even those who are grumpy.

Difficulty: ●●○○
Prep Time: 30 minutes
Yield: 2 drinks
Dietary Notes: Vegetarian

Equipment: Stand mixer with whisk attachment, blender

Strawberry Whipped Cream

¾ cup (177 milliliters) heavy cream

2 tablespoons (2 grams) powdered sugar

2½ tablespoons (30 grams) strawberry powder

2 drops pink food dye

Taro Layer

2½ cups (592 milliliters) cold green tea

⅓ cup (65 grams) taro powder

½ cup (118 milliliters) coconut milk

2 tablespoons (30 milliliters) sweetened condensed milk

10 ice cubes

To make the strawberry whipped cream:

Place all the ingredients into a bowl of a stand mixer. Mix on medium-high speed until the whipped cream forms stiff peaks, about 3 to 5 minutes. Transfer to a piping bag and store in the refrigerator until needed.

To make the taro layer:

1. Combine the green tea, taro powder, coconut milk, and sweetened condensed milk in a blender. Blend until combined.
2. Add the ice cubes and blend until crushed. Pour into two glasses and top with the whipped cream.

Swadloon

Tofu Lettuce Wraps

Try to think of a Swadloon, wrapping itself up with leaves to protect itself from the cold, when you're eating these tofu lettuce wraps. You could even eat these while wrapped up in a blanket—but try not to make a mess!

Difficulty: ●○○○
Prep Time: 30 minutes
Rest Time: 4 hours
Cook Time: 30 minutes
Yield: 2 to 3 servings
Dietary Notes: Vegan

Equipment: Airtight container, cutting board, knife, peeler, grater, small bowl, large nonstick pan

Pickled Carrots and Daikon

½ cup (18 milliliters) rice vinegar
2 cups (473 milliliters) warm water
¼ cup (52 grams) sugar
2 tablespoons (22 grams) kosher salt
2 carrots, julienned
1 small daikon, julienned

Lettuce Wraps

14 ounces (397 grams) firm tofu
¼ cup (59 milliliters) soy sauce
2 tablespoons (45 grams) hoisin sauce
1 tablespoon (15 milliliters) rice vinegar
2 teaspoons (14 grams) honey
1 teaspoon (5 milliliters) sesame oil
1 teaspoon (3 grams) ground turmeric
½ teaspoon (2 grams) ground ginger
½ teaspoon (2 grams) Chinese five-spice powder
2 teaspoons (10 milliliters) canola oil
8 shiitake mushrooms, stemmed and chopped
8 ounces (227 grams) water chestnuts, chopped
6 garlic cloves, minced
1 tablespoon (6 grams) grated fresh ginger
2 scallions, chopped
1 head butter lettuce

To make the pickled carrots and daikon:

1. Combine the rice vinegar, warm water, sugar, and salt in a large airtight container. Add the carrots and daikon radish into the container. If the carrots and daikon are not covered, add additional rice vinegar.

2. Cover and place in the refrigerator for at least 4 hours. The longer they are left to pickle, the more flavorful the carrots and daikon will become. The pickled carrots and daikon can be stored in the refrigerator for about 2 weeks.

To make the lettuce wraps:

1. Wrap the tofu in a paper towel. Place between two plates and top with a heavy object. Allow to rest for 5 minutes to remove excess liquid.

2. Combine the soy sauce, hoisin sauce, rice vinegar, honey, sesame oil, turmeric, ground ginger, and Chinese five-spice powder in a small bowl. Set aside.

3. Heat a large nonstick pan with 1 teaspoon of canola oil over medium-high heat. Add the tofu and cook until all sides have turned golden brown, about 5 minutes. Transfer to a plate.

4. Add the remaining 1 teaspoon of canola oil and add the shiitake mushrooms and water chestnuts. Allow to cook until the mushrooms have softened, about 3 minutes. Toss the garlic, fresh ginger, and scallions in and cook for another 2 minutes, until the garlic becomes aromatic.

5. Add the tofu and the sauce mixture. Mix together to fully coat the tofu. Cook until the liquid has reduced by half, about 5 to 8 minutes. Remove from the heat and transfer to a bowl to serve.

6. To make a portion, take a piece of butter lettuce and top with the pickled vegetables and tofu.

Darumaka

Tomato Soup

Enjoy this soup when it's nice and hot, and you'll have a warm belly, just like Darumaka. But if you eat too much and get too full, you may fall asleep like Darumaka as well!

Difficulty: ●●○○
Prep Time: 30 minutes
Cook Time: 1½ hours
Yield: 4 servings
Dietary Notes: Vegetarian

Equipment: Knife, cutting board, large bowl, large baking sheet, parchment paper, medium pot, blender

Cheddar Croutons

1 baguette, cut into 1-inch (2½-centimeter) cubes
½ cup (118 milliliters) olive oil
1 teaspoon (4 grams) garlic powder
½ teaspoon (2 grams) kosher salt
5 ounces (143 grams) cheddar cheese, finely grated

Tomato Soup

3 tablespoons (45 milliliters) olive oil, plus more for greasing
Kosher salt
Ground black pepper
3 pounds (1⅓ kilograms) tomatoes, quartered
18 garlic cloves, chopped
½ teaspoon (3 grams) red pepper flakes
1 tablespoon (12 grams) onion powder
2 cups (473 milliliters) vegetable stock

To make the cheddar croutons:

1. Preheat oven to 350°F (177°C). Combine the baguette pieces, olive oil, garlic powder, and salt in a large bowl and toss until combined. Transfer to a large baking sheet, with parchment paper, in a single layer. Sprinkle the cheddar cheese on top of the pieces of bread.

2. Bake for 10 minutes. Toss, then bake for another 5 to 10 minutes, or until they are golden brown. Allow to cool completely.

3. The croutons can be stored in an airtight container at room temperature for up to 1 week.

To make the tomato soup:

1. Preheat oven to 400°F (204°C). In a large bowl, combine olive oil, salt, and pepper. Add the tomatoes and toss to coat. Place the tomatoes onto a large baking sheet and into the oven to roast for 45 minutes, until tender and slightly charred.

2. Place a medium pot over medium heat and coat with olive oil. Add the garlic. Cook until the garlic has turned golden brown, about 8 to 10 minutes. Add the red pepper flakes and onion powder. Cook for another 3 minutes, or until fragrant.

3. Add the roasted tomatoes and vegetable stock to the pot. Bring this combination to a boil. Carefully transfer to a blender and blend until smooth. Return the mixture to the pot and heat back up.

4. Split into 4 serving bowls and serve with croutons.

note: **Serve the croutons on the side and place a few of them on top of the soup. Allow them to soften and absorb the soup.**

Crustle
Parfaits

These parfaits are modeled after the boulders that Crustle carry around with them. The layering is up to you, so make sure to personalize it to your liking! But be sure to eat your parfait, not wear it.

Difficulty: ●●○○
Prep Time: 1 hour
Rest Time: 4 hours
Cook Time: 30 minutes
Yield: 4 parfaits, plus extra cookies
Dietary Notes: Vegetarian

Equipment: Small bowl, stand mixer with paddle attachment, large baking sheet, parchment paper, spatula, medium bowl, medium saucepan, whisk

Peanut Butter Cookies

1¼ cups (156 grams) all-purpose flour
1 teaspoon (4 grams) baking powder
½ teaspoon (2 grams) kosher salt
1 cup (240 grams) smooth peanut butter
½ cup (112 grams) unsalted butter, room temperature
2 tablespoons (42 grams) honey
⅓ cup (65 grams) light brown sugar
⅓ cup (75 grams) sugar
1 egg, room temperature
5 ounces (142 grams) peanut butter chips

Chocolate Cookies

1½ cups (187 grams) all-purpose flour
¼ cup (28 grams) black chocolate powder
1 teaspoon (4 grams) baking powder
½ teaspoon (2 grams) kosher salt
½ cup (112 grams) unsalted butter, room temperature
⅓ cup (65 grams) sugar
⅓ cup (75 grams) light brown sugar
1 teaspoon (5 milliliters) vanilla extract
1 egg, room temperature
5 ounces (142 grams) dark chocolate chips

Chocolate Pudding

2 egg yolks
½ cup (100 grams) sugar, divided
2 tablespoons (18 grams) cornstarch
2 cups (473 milliliters) milk, divided
1 tablespoon (7 grams) cocoa powder
¼ teaspoon (1 gram) kosher salt
5 ounces (142 grams) milk chocolate, melted
1 tablespoon (15 milliliters) vanilla extract
2 tablespoons (28 grams) unsalted butter, halved

To make the peanut butter cookies:

1. Preheat oven to 350°F (177°C). Combine the flour, baking powder, and salt in a small bowl. Set aside. Place the peanut butter, butter, and honey in a bowl of a stand mixer. Mix until smooth.
2. Add both sugars and mix until smooth. Add the egg and mix until just combined. Add the flour mixture and whip together until it just comes together. Fold in the peanut butter chips.
3. Prepare a large baking sheet with parchment paper. Take about 1 tablespoon (25 grams) of the dough at a time, place on the baking sheet, and press each down into a cookie shape. Place in the oven to bake for 10 to 13 minutes, or until golden brown.

To make the chocolate cookies:

1. Preheat oven to 350°F (177°C). Combine the flour, black chocolate powder, baking powder, and salt in a small bowl. Set aside. Place the butter in a bowl of a stand mixer. Mix until smooth.
2. Add both sugars and mix until smooth. Add the vanilla extract and egg and mix until just combined. Add the flour mixture and whip together until it just comes together. Fold in the dark chocolate chips.
3. Prepare a large baking sheet with parchment paper. Take about 1 tablespoon (25 grams) of the dough at a time, place on the baking sheet, and press each down into a cookie shape. Place in the oven to bake for 14 to 16 minutes, or until the center is set and firm.

To make the chocolate pudding:

1. Combine the egg yolks, ¼ cup (50 grams) sugar, and cornstarch in a medium bowl. Whisk in ¼ cup of milk and set the bowl aside. Whisk together the remaining 1¾ cups milk, the remaining ¼ cup sugar, cocoa powder, and salt in a medium saucepan. Place over medium-high heat. Get the mixture hot enough to right before it starts to boil. Reduce the heat to low.
2. Scoop out a ½ cup of the cocoa mixture and place it in the bowl with the egg yolks. Whisk the contents in the bowl. Add another ½ cup of cocoa mixture to the bowl while still whisking. Repeat this one last time.
3. Slowly add the mixture into the saucepan. Whisk everything together until it thickens.

> **note: This step should take about 5 to 10 minutes. You'll get an arm workout, but it'll eventually come together. It might even make you as strong as Crustle.**

4. Once the base has thickened, remove it from the heat. Stir in the melted chocolate. Add the vanilla extract and butter. Place the pudding into an airtight container and allow to cool to room temperature. Place in the refrigerator for 4 hours before setting up the parfait.
5. To assemble a parfait, take a large bowl or cup and crumble a layer of the chocolate cookies on the bottom. Press it down into a smooth layer. Top with a portion of the pudding. Add a layer of crumbled peanut butter cookies. Top again with another portion of pudding. Top with either a layer of crumbed chocolate cookies or peanut butter cookies.

Stunfisk

Flatbreads

No other food could represent the flatness of a Stunfisk more than a flatbread. And with different recipes, your flatbread can look like whichever Stunfisk is your favorite!

Difficulty: ●●○○
Prep Time: 1 hour
Rest Time: 2 hours
Cook Time: 30 minutes
Yield: 10 flatbreads
Dietary Notes: Vegetarian

Equipment: Food processor, stand mixer with dough hook attachment, medium bowl, rolling pin, large skillet

Black Sesame Hummus

15½ ounces (440 grams) canned chickpeas, drained and rinsed
2 tablespoons (38 grams) shiro miso
⅓ cup (45 grams) black sesame seeds
1 tablespoon (21 grams) honey
2 garlic cloves
2 tablespoons (30 milliliters) lemon juice
2 tablespoons (30 milliliters) water
1 tablespoon (15 milliliters) olive oil

Dessert Flatbread

¾ cup (177 milliliters) warm water
½ teaspoon (2½ milliliters) vanilla extract
1 tablespoon (15 milliliters) olive oil
2 tablespoons (28 grams) sugar
1 teaspoon (5 grams) active dry yeast
2 cups (325 grams) all-purpose flour
1 teaspoon (4 grams) ground cardamom
½ teaspoon (2 grams) kosher salt
Chocolate hazelnut spread for topping
Sliced banana for topping

Savory Flatbread

¼ cup (32 grams) black sesame seeds
1 tablespoon (21 grams) honey
¾ cup (177 milliliters) warm water
1 tablespoon (15 milliliters) olive oil
2 tablespoons (28 grams) sugar
1 teaspoon (5 grams) active dry yeast
2 cups (325 grams) all-purpose flour
1 teaspoon (4 grams) kosher salt
Black sesame hummus for topping
Fresh mozzarella for topping
Arugula for topping
Mini tomatoes for topping
Balsamic vinegar for topping

To make the black sesame hummus:

Place all the ingredients in a food processor. Pulse until the mixture is smooth. If the mixture is too thick to mix, add 1 teaspoon of water at a time. Transfer to an airtight container and store in the refrigerator. The hummus can be stored for up to 1 week.

To make the dessert flatbread:

1. Combine the water, vanilla extract, olive oil, sugar, and yeast in the bowl of a stand mixer. Whisk together and set aside for 10 minutes to allow the yeast to get frothy. Combine the all-purpose flour, cardamom, and salt in a medium bowl.

2. Add a third of the flour mixture to the stand mixer bowl. Mix at low speed until the dough just starts to come together. Add another third of the flour mixture and keep mixing. Repeat with the last third and mix until the dough is smooth and tacky. If the dough is too sticky, add 1 tablespoon of all-purpose flour until it becomes tacky. Knead the dough for 5 minutes.

3. Transfer the dough ball into an oiled bowl and toss the dough in the oil until all sides are covered. Cover the bowl with plastic wrap and let the dough rest until it has doubled in size, about 2 hours.

4. Lightly flour a countertop and place the dough on the counter. Lightly pat and divide the dough into 5 equal pieces. Tuck in the sides and form each of the pieces into a ball. Cover the dough with a towel and let it rest for 30 minutes.

5. Working on a lightly floured countertop, take a ball and pat down with your hands. With a rolling pin, roll out into the shape of Stunfisk, about 9 inches (23 centimeters) long.

6. Place a large skillet over medium-high heat. Make sure the skillet is hot. Take a rolled-out piece of dough and flip it onto the skillet. Cook until the disk begins to turn golden brown, about 2 to 3 minutes. Flip and repeat on the other side, about 2 minutes. Place the cooked flatbread on a plate and cover with a kitchen towel. Repeat with the remaining disks. To store, allow the flatbreads to cool completely and place them in a resealable bag. They will remain fresh for up to 4 days.

7. To assemble the flatbread, while the flatbread is warm, spread a generous amount of chocolate hazelnut spread and top with sliced bananas.

continued on the next page

To make the savory flatbread:

1. Place the black sesame seeds in a food processor and pulse until smooth. Add honey until it forms a smooth paste.

2. Combine the black sesame, water, olive oil, sugar, and yeast in the bowl of a stand mixer. Whisk together and set aside for 10 minutes to allow the yeast to get frothy. Combine the all-purpose flour and salt in a medium bowl.

3. Add a third of the flour mixture to the stand mixer bowl. Mix at low speed until the dough just starts to come together. Add another third of the flour mixture and keep mixing. Repeat with the last third and mix until the dough is smooth and tacky. If the dough is too sticky, add 1 tablespoon of all-purpose flour until it becomes tacky. Knead the dough for 5 minutes.

4. Transfer the dough ball into an oiled bowl and toss the dough in the oil until all sides are covered. Cover the bowl with plastic wrap and let the dough rest until it has doubled in size, about 2 hours.

5. Lightly flour a countertop and place the dough on the counter. Lightly pat and divide the dough into 5 equal pieces. Tuck in the sides and form each of the pieces into a ball. Cover the dough with a towel and let it rest for 30 minutes.

6. Working on a lightly floured countertop, take a ball and pat down with your hands. With a rolling pin, roll out into the shape of Stunfisk, about 9 inches (23 centimeters) long.

7. Place a skillet over medium-high heat. Make sure the skillet is hot. Take a rolled-out piece of dough and flip it onto the skillet. Cook until the disk begins to turn golden brown, about 2 to 3 minutes. Flip and repeat on the other side, about 2 minutes. Place the cooked flatbread on a plate and cover with a kitchen towel. Repeat with the remaining disks. To store, allow the flatbreads to cool completely and place them into a resealable bag. They will remain fresh for up to 4 days.

8. To assemble the flatbread, while the flatbread is warm, spread a generous amount of the black sesame hummus. Top with fresh mozzarella, arugula, mini tomatoes, and balsamic vinegar.

Kalos Region

Pyroar

Gogoat

Pancham

Sylveon

Dedenne

Sliggoo

Pyroar

Bruschetta

Pyroar's fire breath can get to over 10,000°F, but we won't need nearly that much heat to prepare these bruschetta. A typical kitchen oven will do the job nicely.

Difficulty: ●○○○
Prep Time: 30 minutes
Cook Time: 1 hour
Yield: 15 to 20 bruschettas
Dietary Notes: Vegan

Equipment: Knife, cutting board, large baking sheet, small nonstick pan, medium bowl

2 yellow bell peppers, halved and seeded
Kosher salt
Ground black pepper
1 tablespoon (15 milliliters) olive oil, plus more for brushing
5 garlic cloves, minced
11 ½ ounces (330 grams tomatoes), chopped
4 to 6 Calabrian chile peppers
5 grams fresh basil, thinly sliced
1 teaspoon (5 milliliters) balsamic vinegar
1 baguette, cut into medium slices

1. Heat oven to 450°F (232°C). Place the bell peppers on a baking sheet, skin side up. Brush with olive oil and season with salt and pepper. Bake in the oven for 30 to 40 minutes, until it has softened and the skin has charred slightly. Remove the bell peppers from the oven and allow to cool.
2. Remove the skin and discard. Cut the bell peppers into thick slices and set aside. Reduce the oven to 400°F (204°C).
3. Place a nonstick small pan over medium-high heat. Add ½ tablespoon olive oil and garlic. Cook until the garlic is golden brown, about 3 to 5 minutes. Once cooked, place the cooked garlic in a medium bowl. Add the tomatoes, Calabrian chile peppers, basil, the remaining olive oil, and balsamic vinegar. Season with salt and pepper.
4. Place the baguette slices on a large baking sheet and bake for 4 minutes. Flip and bake for another 4 minutes, or until crispy and golden. Once baked, take each of the baked slices and brush olive oil over them. Place a portion of the tomato mixture on top of each slice. Top with a piece of bell pepper.

Gogoat
Breakfast Burritos

Gogoats are always working hard, traveling along mountain trails with their herds or their rider. If you've got plans to explore the outdoors, a hearty breakfast like these breakfast burritos is a great way to prepare for fun activities outside.

Difficulty: ●●○○
Prep Time: 30 minutes
Cook Time: 30 minutes
Yield: 4 servings
Dietary Notes: Vegetarian, nondairy

Equipment: Vegetable peeler, box grater, knife, cutting board, medium bowl, 2 medium nonstick pans

Hash Browns

1 large russet potato, peeled and shredded
1 tablespoon (10 grams) garlic powder
2 teaspoons (6 grams) onion powder
1 tablespoon (15 milliliters) olive oil
Kosher salt
Ground black pepper

Burritos

2 teaspoons (10 milliliters) canola oil
8 baby portobello mushrooms, sliced
6 ounces (170 grams) spinach
4 eggs
Four 8-inch (20-centimeter) whole grain tortillas
8 ounces (226 grams) refried beans, warmed up
1 avocado, sliced
Fresh cilantro, chopped

To make the hash browns:

1. Combine the shredded potato, garlic powder, and onion powder in a medium bowl. Heat a medium nonstick pan with olive oil over medium-high heat. Add the shredded potato. Generously season with salt and pepper. Allow the potato to cook until the bottom has browned, about 5 to 8 minutes.

2. Carefully flip the potato. Season with salt and pepper again. Cook until the other side has browned completely, about 5 minutes. Split into 4 portions. Set aside.

To make the burritos:

1. Heat a medium nonstick pan with 1 teaspoon (5 milliliters) canola oil over medium heat. Add the mushrooms and cook until golden brown, about 10 to 15 minutes. Remove from the pan and set aside. Add the spinach and cook until just wilted, about 1 minute.

2. Crack and scramble the eggs in a medium bowl. Heat a medium nonstick pan over medium heat with the remaining 1 teaspoon canola oil. Pour the scrambled egg into the pan and let it cook fully, about 2 to 3 minutes. Split into 4 portions and set aside.

3. Heat up the tortillas and prepare to assemble. Take a tortilla and add a layer of refried beans. Top with the mushrooms, scrambled eggs, hash browns, avocado slices, and chopped cilantro and carefully wrap. Heat a medium nonstick pan over medium-high heat. Place the wrapped burrito, crease side down. Cook until golden brown, about 2 minutes. Flip and cook until golden brown again, about 2 minutes. Repeat with the remaining tortillas.

note: There are many vegetables that would work well in this burrito. Pick your favorite to make these your own!

Pancham

Rice Bowls

Pancham always seems to be glaring at others, but sometimes it forgets to keep up the tough exterior and smiles. When you decorate your rice bowls, try your best Pancham impersonation and then decorate the bowl to look the same way.

Difficulty: ●●○○
Prep Time: 30 minutes
Rest Time: 10 minutes
Cook Time: 20 minutes
Yield: 4 servings
Dietary Notes: Vegan

Equipment: Knife, cutting board, large nonstick pan, small bowl

Sauce

¼ cup (59 milliliters) water
1 teaspoon (3 grams) potato starch
2 tablespoons (30 milliliters) soy sauce
1 teaspoon (5 milliliters) white vinegar
1 teaspoon (5 milliliters) sesame oil
2 tablespoons (30 grams) maple syrup

Rice Bowl

16 ounces (454 grams) firm tofu
2 teaspoons (10 milliliters) canola oil
6 shiitake mushrooms, sliced
8 ounces (227 grams) green beans
1 eggplant, cut into bite-size pieces
6 ounces (170 grams) baby broccoli, cut into bite-size pieces
8 ounces (227 grams) bean sprouts
Kosher salt
Pepper
3 cups (424 grams) cooked rice
2 sheets nori
4 Thai basil leaves

To make the sauce:

Combine the ingredients in a small bowl and set aside.

To make the rice bowl:

1. Place the tofu between two plates and top with a heavy object. Allow this to rest for 10 minutes to remove excess liquid.

2. Heat a large nonstick pan with 1 teaspoon canola oil over medium-high heat. Add the tofu and cook until all sides have slightly browned, about 5 to 8 minutes. Transfer to a plate.

3. Add the remaining 1 teaspoon canola oil and add the shiitake mushrooms, green beans, eggplant, and baby broccoli. Cook until the vegetables have softened, about 5 to 8 minutes. Add the tofu and toss to mix in.

4. Add the sauce, toss to coat everything, and cook until the sauce has reduced and thickened, about 3 minutes. Add the bean sprouts and cook for another 2 minutes. Season with salt and pepper. Remove from the heat and set aside to serve.

5. Prepare the cooked rice by shaping it like Pancham's face. Use nori pieces to add the details of Pancham's face. Finally, add a Thai basil leaf to mimic the small leaf in Pancham's mouth. Serve the portion of rice with the stir-fried vegetables.

Sylveon

Strawberry Shortcake

Sylveon is capable of stopping any conflict, releasing enmity-erasing waves and bringing peace to those around it. If Sylveon isn't around when you get into trouble, a bite of these minty strawberry shortcakes is a perfect substitute to help everyone relax.

Difficulty: ●●○○
Prep Time: 30 minutes
Rest Time: 1 hour
Cook Time: 30 minutes
Yield: 12 strawberry shortcakes
Dietary Notes: Vegetarian

Equipment: Medium bowl, large baking sheet, parchment paper, stand mixer with whisk attachment, small bowl, wire rack

Biscuits

3 cups (465 grams) all-purpose flour
2 tablespoons (27 grams) sugar
1 tablespoon (9 grams) baking powder
2 teaspoons (8 grams) kosher salt
1 cup (224 grams) unsalted butter, cubed and chilled in the freezer for at least 20 minutes
1¼ cups (296 milliliters) buttermilk, chilled
2 tablespoons (28 grams) unsalted butter, melted
Coarse sugar for sprinkling

Mint Whipped Cream

1½ cups (355 milliliters) heavy cream
1 tablespoon (9 grams) confectioners' sugar
½ teaspoon (2½ milliliters) peppermint extract
1 pinch kosher salt
3 drops light blue food dye

Sweetened Strawberries

1 pound (454 grams) fresh strawberries
2 tablespoons (25 grams) sugar

To make the biscuits:

1. Combine flour, sugar, baking powder, and salt in a medium bowl. Add the cubed butter and combine with your hands until it resembles coarse cornmeal. Place in the refrigerator and let rest for 15 minutes.

2. Remove from the refrigerator, add the buttermilk, and stir until the dough barely comes together. Transfer to a floured countertop and work until the dough just comes together. Roll the dough into a 1-inch-tall rectangle. Fold the top third of the dough toward you. Next, fold the bottom third over the first fold. Reroll the dough again and repeat the fold. Reroll the dough once more. Cut the dough into 12 triangle pieces.

3. Preheat oven to 425°F (218°C). Place the pieces on a large baking sheet with parchment paper. Place in the freezer for 20 minutes. Remove and brush each of the biscuits with melted butter and sprinkle on coarse sugar. Bake for 15 to 20 minutes, or until golden brown. Transfer to a wire rack and allow to cool.

To make the mint whipped cream:

1. Place the heavy cream, confectioners' sugar, peppermint extract, and salt into a bowl of a stand mixer. Mix on medium high speed until the whipped cream forms stiff peaks, about 3 to 5 minutes.

2. Split the whipped cream in half. Add the light blue food dye to one half and fold in.

3. Store in the refrigerator until needed.

To make the sweetened strawberries:

Place the strawberries and sugar in a small bowl and allow to rest for 30 minutes.

For assembly:

1. Cut a biscuit in half and place the bottom piece on a plate. Top with light blue whipped cream. Place a generous portion of strawberries on top.

2. Top with the white whipped cream and place the biscuit on top.

3. Decorate with melted pink chocolate (optional), additional whipped cream, and strawberries.

Dedenne **Ramen**

Dedenne can't generate much electricity on its own, but it always knows where to go to store up energy for its next Pokémon battle. A heaping bowl of ramen is a great source of energy for those on the go!

Difficulty: ●●●○
Prep Time: 30 minutes
Rest Time: 24 hours
Cook Time: 40 minutes
Yield: 4 to 6 servings
Dietary Notes: Vegetarian

Equipment: Medium pot, medium bowl, small nonstick pan, small bowl, large pot

Ajitsuke Tamago

4 eggs
½ cup (118 milliliters) soy sauce
¼ cup (58 grams) sugar
¼ cup (59 milliliters) water
2 tablespoons (50 grams) vegetarian oyster sauce

Curry Broth

¼ cup (40 grams) all-purpose flour
1½ tablespoons (9 grams) ground garam masala
1½ tablespoons (9 grams) ground turmeric
1 teaspoon (2 grams) ground fennel
1 teaspoon (3 grams) ground fenugreek seeds
½ teaspoon (1 gram) ground cinnamon
½ teaspoon (1 gram) ground cayenne pepper
5 tablespoons (70 grams) unsalted butter
3 tablespoons (85 grams) tomato paste
2 teaspoons (12 grams) tonkatsu sauce
1 tablespoon (21 grams) honey
1 tablespoon (15 milliliters) canola oil
½ red onion, sliced
5 shiitake mushrooms, thinly sliced
5 cups (1,183 milliliters) vegetable broth
2 golden potatoes, peeled and cut into bite-size pieces
2 carrots, peeled and cut into bite-size pieces
¼ cup (59 milliliters) soy sauce

For assembly, per serving

1 portion ramen noodles
2 pieces aburaage tofu, sliced
1 ajitsuke tamago, halved
1 scallion, sliced
Nori for garnishing

To make the ajitsuke tamago:

1. Bring a medium pot of water to a boil. Gently place the eggs in the pot, cover, and cook for 6½ minutes. Once cooked, immediately take the pot off the stove and place under cold running water. Move the contents to a medium bowl with ice cubes and water. Let rest for 5 minutes. Carefully remove the shells from the eggs.

2. Mix the soy sauce, sugar, water, and vegetarian oyster sauce in a resealable bag. Add the eggs. Seal and make sure the eggs are fully covered. Place in the refrigerator and marinate for at least 24 hours. The eggs can be stored in the refrigerator for up to 3 days.

To make the curry broth:

1. Combine the flour, garam masala, turmeric, fennel, fenugreek, cinnamon, and cayenne pepper in a small bowl. In a small nonstick pan, over medium-high heat, melt the butter. Add the flour and spices to the melted butter.

2. Mix together until the flour has absorbed all the butter. Add the tomato paste, tonkatsu sauce, and honey. Once combined, turn off the heat and set the roux aside.

3. Heat a large pot with canola oil over medium-high heat. Add the onions and shiitake mushrooms. Cook until softened, about 5 minutes.

4. Add the vegetable broth, potatoes, and carrots. Bring to a boil and then reduce the heat to have the liquid at a simmer. Place the lid slightly ajar and simmer for 20 minutes.

5. Take a small portion of the roux and place it in a ladle. Place the ladle in the liquid of the pot and slowly mix in the roux. Repeat in small portions until all the roux is added to the pot. Add the soy sauce. Let simmer for 5 minutes.

To serve the ramen bowls:

Prepare a serving of ramen noodles and the broth with potatoes and carrots. Top with the aburaage, ajitsuke tamago, scallions, and nori.

note: If you want to shape this like Dedenne, cut the aburaage in the shape of Dedenne and place on the bowl. Make sure to leave a portion of the ramen noodles to represent the belly. It is also extremely helpful to precut the nori into the shape of the whiskers and eyes ahead of time.

Sliggoo

Purple Cauliflower Soup

Sliggoo isn't very strong, but it's important to handle with great care. You'll want to take the same care carrying this cauliflower and potato soup, which is just the thing to satisfy your hunger.

Difficulty: ●●○○
Prep Time: 30 minutes
Cook Time: 1½ hours
Yield: 4 to 6 servings
Dietary Notes: Vegan

Equipment: 2 large baking sheets, aluminum foil, 2 medium bowls, 2 medium pots, blender

Light Purple Soup

1 head purple cauliflower, cut into bite-size pieces
2 tablespoons (30 milliliters) olive oil
Kosher salt
Ground black pepper
2 shallots, chopped
3 garlic cloves, minced
1½ cups (355 milliliters) vegetable broth
½ cup (59 milliliters) coconut milk

Dark Purple Soup

Nonstick cooking spray for greasing
1 pound (454 grams) purple sweet potato, peeled and cut into bite-size pieces
2 tablespoons (30 milliliters) olive oil
Kosher salt
Ground black pepper
½ red onion, chopped
3 garlic cloves, minced
2 cups (473 milliliters) vegetable broth
Fresh chives, finely chopped, for garnishing

To start the dark purple soup:

1. Preheat oven to 375°F (191°C). Prepare 2 large baking sheets with aluminum foil and nonstick cooking spray.
2. Place the purple sweet potato in a medium bowl. Add 1 tablespoon (15 milliliters) olive oil and toss until coated.
3. Transfer to one of the baking sheets and generously season with salt and pepper. Place in the oven and cook for 45 to 60 minutes, until softened and cooked through.

To make the light purple soup:

1. When the sweet potatoes are about halfway through their cooking time, place the cauliflower in a medium bowl and toss with 1 tablespoon (15 milliliters) olive oil until coated.
2. Transfer to the other baking sheet and generously season with salt and pepper. Place in the oven and cook for 25 to 30 minutes, until golden, softened, and cooked through.
3. Place a medium pot with the remaining 1 tablespoon olive oil over medium-high heat. Add the shallot and garlic and cook until softened, about 5 minutes. Add the cauliflower and toss to coat.
4. Add the vegetable broth and bring to a boil. Reduce the heat and simmer for 20 minutes. Remove from the heat and transfer to a blender.
5. Blend until smooth. Return to the pot and add the coconut milk. Heat until everything is warmed up.

To make the dark purple soup:

1. Place a medium pot with the remaining 1 tablespoon olive oil over medium-high heat. Add the red onion and garlic and cook until softened, about 3 minutes. Add the sweet potatoes and toss to coat.
2. Add the vegetable broth and bring to a boil. Reduce the heat and simmer for 20 minutes. Remove from the heat and transfer to a blender.
3. Blend until smooth. Return to the pot and heat until everything is warmed up.

For assembly:

1. To serve, pour a portion of each of the soups into a bowl and garnish with freshly chopped chives.

Alola Region

Incineroar

Mudbray

Bewear

Tsareena

Bruxish

Alolan Exeggutor

Incineroar

Eggplant Parmigiana Sandwiches

You won't have Incineroar's flames around your waist after eating these deliciously spicy sandwiches, but the heat will still warm your belly. Show off your best fighting spirit after eating one!

Difficulty: ●●○○
Prep Time: 45 minutes
Rest Time: 15 minutes
Cook Time: 40 minutes
Yield: 3 sandwiches
Dietary Notes: Vegetarian

Equipment: Medium saucepan, large deep-frying pan, large baking sheet, small bowl, medium bowl

Spicy Marinara

3 tablespoons (45 milliliters) olive oil
6 garlic cloves, minced
½ onion, minced
2 tablespoons (28 grams) tomato paste
1 tablespoon (14 grams) gochujang
1 teaspoon (3 grams) sweet paprika
2 teaspoons (6 grams) crushed red pepper flakes
1 tablespoon (12 grams) sugar
One 28-ounce (794-gram) can whole tomatoes
Kosher salt
Ground black pepper

Fried Eggplant

1 eggplant, thickly sliced
½ cup (80 grams) all-purpose flour
1 teaspoon (4 grams) kosher salt, plus more for salting the eggplant
1 teaspoon (2 grams) ground black pepper
½ tablespoon (5 grams) garlic powder
1 pinch cayenne
2 eggs
1 tablespoon (15 milliliters) milk
1 cup (70 grams) panko breadcrumbs
½ cup (70 grams) regular breadcrumbs
1 teaspoon (2 grams) dried oregano
1 teaspoon (2 grams) dried basil
Peanut oil for frying

Per Serving

1 Italian sandwich roll
2 whole black garlic cloves
¼ cup (52 grams) unsalted butter, room temperature
3 slices fried eggplant
Spicy marinara for topping
Fresh mozzarella for topping
Fresh basil for topping

To make the spicy marinara:

1. Heat a medium saucepan with olive oil over medium-high heat. Add the garlic and onion. Cook until softened, about 5 minutes. Add the tomato paste and gochujang and allow to cook for another 2 minutes.

2. Add the paprika, red pepper flakes, and sugar. Mix to combine. Take the whole tomatoes and crush them with your hands. Add them to the pan. Reduce the heat to medium-low and simmer for 30 minutes. Season with salt and pepper. Set aside until you are ready to put the sandwiches together.

To make the eggplant:

1. Place the cut eggplant into a strainer and cover generously with salt. Place a plate on top and add some weight. Let it sit for 15 minutes. This step is done to remove some of the liquid in the eggplant. Do not skip it! Your eggplant will be soggy if you do.

2. Combine the flour, salt, pepper, garlic powder, and cayenne on a plate. Combine the egg and milk in a medium bowl. Combine the panko, regular breadcrumbs, oregano, and basil on another plate.

3. Take the eggplant and pat with a paper towel to remove the excess liquid. Take one of the eggplant slices and dip it in the flour mixture. Cover it well in flour. Dip it in the egg mixture. Cover it completely. Let any excess liquid drip off the eggplant and then place it in the breadcrumb mixture.

4. In a large deep-frying pan, add ½ inch of peanut oil and let the oil heat up to roughly 360°F (182°C). It is ready when you add a small piece of panko and the oil sizzles. Add the breaded eggplant and fry for 3 minutes per side, or until golden brown. Once cooked, transfer onto a plate with a paper towel to drain excess oil. Repeat until all the eggplant is cooked.

For assembly:

1. Preheat oven broiler. Slice the roll in half and place on a large baking sheet. Combine the black garlic and butter in a small bowl. Spread the inside of each of the buns with the combined butter. Place under the broiler and toast until the buns have crisped up, about 2 minutes.

> **note:** **This is more butter than you'll need for a single serving. This mixture can be stored in an airtight container for up to 1 week.**

2 To assemble, place a small amount of spicy marinara on the bottom portion of the roll. Top with the fried eggplant, more sauce, fresh mozzarella, and basil. Place the roll top and serve.

Mudbray
Babka

Chocolate babka can be a messy meal to make, so be sure to clean up afterward. You may want to feel like a Mudbray and get chocolate all over your hands, but you'll just make cleanup that much harder.

Difficulty: ●●●○
Prep Time: 1 hour
Rest Time: 2 hours
Cook Time: 20 minutes
Yield: 6 buns
Dietary Notes: Vegetarian

Equipment: Stand mixer with dough hook attachment, knife, large bowl, medium saucepan, large baking sheet, parchment paper

Dough

¾ cup (177 milliliters) milk, heated to 100°F (38°C)
½ tablespoon (5 grams) active dry yeast
3½ cups (545 grams) all-purpose flour
½ teaspoon (1 gram) grated nutmeg
¼ cup (59 grams) sugar
1 teaspoon (4 grams) kosher salt
2 eggs
1 teaspoon (5 milliliters) vanilla extract
6 tablespoons (84 grams) unsalted butter, room temperature

Filling

⅓ cup (75 grams) unsalted butter
⅓ cup (70 grams) chopped dark chocolate
3 tablespoons (27 grams) cocoa powder
2 tablespoons (30 grams) almond butter
⅓ cup (45 grams) confectioners' sugar
2 teaspoons (8 grams) kosher salt

Syrup

3 tablespoons (39 milliliters) water
¼ cup (59 grams) sugar

To make the dough:

1. Combine the milk and yeast. Allow the yeast to bloom, about 5 minutes. Combine the flour, nutmeg, sugar, and salt in a bowl of a stand mixer. Add the yeast mixture, eggs, and vanilla extract. Mix until it just comes together.
2. While the dough begins to knead, add the butter 1 tablespoon at a time. Knead the dough for 5 minutes. If the dough is too sticky, add 1 tablespoon of flour at a time. If it is too dry, add 1 tablespoon of milk at a time. Transfer to an oiled bowl, cover, and let rest for 1 hour, or until it has doubled in size.

To make the filling:

1. Place the butter in a medium saucepan over medium heat. Allow the butter to melt. Once melted, add the remaining ingredients for the filling and mix together until the chocolate is melted. Remove from the heat and set aside.
2. Transfer the dough to a lightly floured countertop and punch down. Lightly knead for 1 minute. Divide into 6 equal portions and cover with a kitchen towel.
3. Take one of the portions and roll out into an 8-by-5-inch (20-by-12½-centimeter) rectangle. Take a generous portion of the filling and spread it on the dough, leaving a ¼-inch (6-millimeter) border. Tightly roll the dough and pinch the seam to seal.
4. Cut the roll in half lengthwise, but not all the way through, leaving one end connected on the bottom. Turn the cut ends upward. Tightly braid the two pieces together and pinch the end of the braid together. Shape the braided log into a tight circle and knot the two ends closed. Place on a large baking sheet with parchment paper, leaving 3 inches (7½ centimeters) in between each bun. Repeat steps 3 and 4 with the remaining portions.
5. Once all the buns are set, cover the tray with a kitchen towel and allow to rest for 1 hour, or until risen.

To make the syrup:

1. Combine water and sugar in a medium saucepan over medium-high heat. Mix together. Once the sugar dissolves, reduce the heat to medium-low and simmer for 10 minutes. Remove from the heat and set aside.
2. Preheat oven to 350°F (177°C). Brush each of the buns with the syrup. Place in the oven and bake for 20 minutes, or until golden brown.

Bewear

Raspberry Chocolate Cupcakes

Though sharing a hug with friends is a nice gesture, Bewear's hugs are too powerful. Perhaps it would like to share this tasty cupcake instead.

Difficulty: ●●●○
Prep Time:1 hour
Cook Time: 20 minutes
Yield: 14 to 15 cupcakes
Dietary Notes: Vegetarian

Equipment: Stand mixer with paddle attachment, small bowl, medium bowl, whisk, muffin pan

Dark Chocolate Cupcakes

¼ cup (59 milliliters) hot water
2 tablespoons (36 grams) raspberry jam
¼ cup (35 grams) black cocoa powder
1¼ cups (220 grams) all-purpose flour
1 teaspoon (5 grams) baking powder
½ teaspoon (2 grams) kosher salt
½ cup (112 grams) unsalted butter, room temperature
½ cup (115 grams) sugar
¼ cup (58 grams) brown sugar
3 ounces (85 grams) dark chocolate, melted and cooled
2 eggs
1 teaspoon (5 milliliters) vanilla extract
½ cup (130 grams) sour cream
¼ cup (59 milliliters) heavy cream

Frosting

4 ounces (113 grams) cream cheese, room temperature
¼ cup (56 grams) unsalted butter, room temperature
1 teaspoon (5 milliliters) vanilla extract
3 drops pink food dye
⅓ cup (100 grams) raspberry jam
3 cups (375 grams) confectioners' sugar

To make the dark chocolate cupcakes:

1. Preheat oven to 350°F (177°C). Combine the hot water, raspberry jam, and cocoa powder in a small bowl. Whisk together until smooth. Combine the flour, baking powder, and kosher salt in a medium bowl.

2. Place the butter in a bowl of a stand mixer and mix until creamed and smooth. Add the sugars and melted dark chocolate. Mix until smooth. Add and mix in the eggs one at a time. Add the vanilla extract and cocoa powder mixture and mix until combined.

3. Mix in a third of the flour mixture. Follow that with half of the sour cream. Add another third of the flour mixture and then the remaining sour cream and heavy cream. Finally, mix in the last of the flour.

4. Take your muffin pan and fill them three-fourths of the way up with the batter. Bake for 15 to 20 minutes, or until they pass the toothpick test. Allow the cupcakes to cool completely before dressing them up.

To make the frosting:

1. Place the cream cheese and butter in a bowl of a stand mixer and mix. Add the vanilla extract, pink food dye, and raspberry jam.

2. Once it is well mixed, begin to slowly add the confectioners' sugar. Add until the cream cheese frosting has thickened enough to pipe. Transfer to a pastry bag with a frosting tip of your choice. Frost each of the cupcakes.

Tsareena
Roast Beet Salad

If you want to grow up strong like Tsareena, you'll need a balanced diet with plenty of vegetables. If you had powerful kicks just like Tsareena, think of all the sports and other activities in which you could excel.

Difficulty: ●○○○
Prep Time: 45 minutes
Cook Time: 1 hour
Yield: 4 to 6 servings
Dietary Notes: Vegetarian, gluten-free

Equipment: Medium baking tray, aluminum foil, small bowl, large bowl, cutting board, knife

Roasted Beets

3 red beets, leaves and stems removed
1 tablespoon (15 milliliters) olive oil
Kosher salt
Ground black pepper

Orange Shallot Vinaigrette

1 small shallot, minced
2 garlic cloves, minced
¼ cup (59 milliliters) orange juice
1 tablespoon (6 grams) orange zest
1 tablespoon (15 milliliters) apple cider vinegar
1 tablespoon (21 grams) honey
1 tablespoon (15 grams) Dijon mustard
⅓ cup (79 milliliters) olive oil
Kosher salt
Ground black pepper

Salad

4 ounces (113 grams) spinach
8 ounces (227 grams) arugula
4 ounces (113 grams) goat cheese, crumbled
½ red onion, thinly sliced
4 ounces (113 grams) walnuts, coarsely chopped

To make the roasted beets:

1. Preheat oven to 400°F (204°C). Rub the beets with olive oil. Generously season with salt and pepper. Take one of the beets, place it on a sheet of aluminum foil, and wrap it shut. Repeat with the remaining beets.

2. Place the aluminum wrapped beets on a medium baking tray. Transfer to the oven and roast for 45 to 60 minutes, until tender.

3. Allow the beets to cool before peeling and discarding the skin. Thinly slice the beets into ¼-inch-thick (3-millimeter-thick) bite-size pieces. The sliced beets can be stored in an airtight container in the refrigerator for up to 1 week.

To make the orange shallot vinaigrette:

1. Combine the shallots, garlic, orange juice, orange zest, apple cider vinegar, honey, and Dijon mustard in a small bowl. Let sit for 20 minutes. Whisk in the olive oil and season with salt and pepper to your liking.

2. The vinaigrette can be stored in an airtight container in the refrigerator for up to 1 week. The oil and acid will separate after sitting for a while, so make sure to shake vigorously before serving.

To make the salad:

Combine spinach and arugula in a large bowl and toss until well mixed. Transfer an equal portion to 6 salad bowls. Top each with roasted beets, goat cheese, red onion, and walnuts. Serve with orange shallot vinaigrette.

Bruxish
Slush

Bruxish scales have beautiful patterns, but it's best to observe them from a safe distance, as their sharp, grinding teeth are dangerous. This slush has its own beautiful pattern, and the flavor has a bite to it, but at least it won't be taking a bite out of you!

Difficulty: ●○○○
Prep Time: 30 minutes
Rest Time: 8 hours
Yield: 3 drinks
Dietary Notes: Vegan

Equipment: Two 12-slot ice cube trays, blender

Blue Ice Cubes

7 butterfly pea flowers

1 tablespoon (5 grams) green tea

1 cup (237 milliliters) hot water

Pink Ice Cubes

¼ cup (57 grams) frozen raspberries

1 cup (237 milliliters) hot water

1 drop pink food dye (optional)

Per Serving

4 blue ice cubes

3 pink ice cubes

1 cup (237 milliliters) lemonade

note: **You can use store-bought or Ampharos's Lemonade (page 33). I would recommend leaving out the citric acid so this lemonade isn't as sour.**

To make the blue ice cubes:

1. Place the butterfly pea flowers and green tea in a cup with a strainer. Add the water and let brew for 5 minutes.

2. Strain and transfer to an ice cube tray and allow to cool. Place in the freezer for at least 8 hours before using.

To make the pink ice cubes:

1. Place the raspberries in a cup with a strainer. Add the water and let brew for 5 minutes. Add the pink food dye.

2. Strain and transfer to an ice cube tray and allow to cool. Place in the freezer for at least 8 hours before using.

For assembly:

1. Take the blue ice cubes and place them in a blender. Blend until the ice is crushed. Transfer to a cup.

2. Clean out the blender. Place the pink ice cubes into the blender and blend until the ice is crushed. Place in the same cup with the crushed blue ice.

3. Pour the lemonade into the cup and enjoy.

Alolan Exeggutor

Tall Tropical Slushie

Did you know that blazing sunlight has brought out the true form and powers of this Pokémon? I bet we can make an equally powerful drink by combining three delicious tropical fruits!

Difficulty: ●○○○
Prep Time: 15 minutes
Yield: 1 Alola-size serving or 2 Kanto-size servings
Dietary Notes: Vegan

Equipment: Blender

9 ounces (255 grams) frozen mango chunks
12 ounces (340 grams) frozen pineapple chunks
4 ounces (113 grams) ice
1½ cups (353 milliliters) coconut water

Place all the ingredients in a blender and blend until smooth. If making an Alola-size serving, serve in one large cup. If making a Kanto-size serving, split between two glasses.

Galar Region

Eldegoss

Toxtricity

Centiskorch

Clobbopus

Porpeko

Cufant

Eldegoss

Spinach Mushroom Burger

Eldegoss loves to spread its seeds to the wind to help benefit other Pokémon. You could do the same if you shared these delicious mushroom burgers with friends and family! Although, they are so delicious that you may have second thoughts about sharing after taking a bite.

Difficulty: ●●○○
Prep Time: 30 minutes
Rest Time: 2 hours
Cook Time: 30 minutes
Yield: 6 burgers
Dietary Notes: Vegetarian

Equipment: Large bowl, rolling pin, parchment paper, large pot with steamer basket, stand mixer with dough hook attachment, large baking sheet

Steamed Buns

2 teaspoons (6 grams) active dry yeast
¾ cup (177 milliliters) warm water, plus more for steaming

> **note:** **It is very important that the water is no warmer than 110°F (43°C) because if it is any warmer, it will kill the yeast and not allow the dough to rise. You can use a meat thermometer to check the temperature.**

¼ cup (59 milliliters) canola oil
2¾ cups (410 grams) all-purpose flour
¼ cup (38 grams) cornstarch
1 tablespoon (12 grams) baking powder
¼ cup (60 grams) sugar
2 teaspoons (8 grams) kosher salt
Black sesame seeds for garnishing

Mushroom Burgers

1 shallot, chopped
1 garlic cloves, minced
¼ cup (59 milliliters) balsamic vinegar
3 tablespoons (45 milliliters) olive oil
6 portobello mushrooms, stemmed

Per Serving

1 slice cheddar cheese (optional)
1 mushroom burger
1 steamed bun
Mayonnaise for topping
½ avocado, sliced
Cooked spinach for topping
Arugula for topping

To make the steamed buns:

1. Mix the yeast, water, and canola oil. Allow to rest for 5 minutes or until the yeast becomes active. Combine the flour, cornstarch, baking powder, sugar, and salt in a bowl of a stand mixer. Slowly mix in the liquid with the flour. Mix until it all comes together.

2. Transfer to a lightly floured surface and knead by hand for 5 minutes. Place the dough in an oiled bowl and cover. Let it rest until it doubles in size, about 2 hours.

3. Punch down the dough and roll out into a long tube. Split into 6 equal pieces and form into balls. Place each onto a sheet of parchment paper and place into a steamer basket. Cover and allow to rest for 30 minutes. Lightly wet the tops of each of the rounds and place a few black sesame seeds on.

> **note:** **Press lightly on the sesame seeds so that they stick without the pressure deflating the buns.**

4. Heat a pot that the steamer basket can sit on with water over high heat and bring to a boil. Once boiling, reduce the heat to medium and place the steamer basket on top. Allow to steam for 15 to 20 minutes, until cooked through.

5. Turn off the heat and let sit, covered, for 5 minutes before using the buns. This will help prevent them from shrinking.

To make the mushroom burgers:

1. Combine the shallots, garlic, balsamic vinegar, and olive oil. Place the mushrooms, top side down, on an aluminum covered large baking sheet. Cover the inside of the mushroom with the dressing and allow it to marinade for at least 30 minutes.

2. Preheat oven to 375°F (191°C). Place the mushrooms in the oven and cook for 25 minutes, until the mushrooms are soft and cooked through.

For assembly:

1. If adding a slice of cheddar cheese to your serving, place on top of the cooked mushroom and place under a broiler until it has melted, about 2 minutes.

2. Cut a bun open and cover the bottom portion with mayonnaise. Top that with avocado slices and then the mushroom. Finally, top with the spinach, arugula, and the bun top.

Toxtricity

Blue & Yellow Smoothie

When Toxtricity generates a tremendous amount of electricity, it makes a sound that can resemble a daunting bass guitar. It's best to keep your distance, so enjoy a smoothie that matches your own mood!

Difficulty: ●○○○
Prep Time: 20 minutes
Yield: 2 smoothies
Dietary Notes: Vegan

Equipment: Blender

Purple Layer

1 banana
1 lime, juiced
¾ cup (177 milliliters) coconut milk
1 cup (160 grams) frozen pineapple chunks
½ cup (68 grams) frozen blueberries
½ cup (70 grams) frozen blackberries

Yellow Layer

½ banana
1 lemon, zested and juiced
1 lime, zested and juiced
2 tablespoons (30 milliliters) coconut milk
½ cup (80 grams) frozen pineapple chunks
1 teaspoon (5 grams) citric acid

Blue Layer

½ banana
⅓ cup (79 milliliters) coconut milk
½ cup (80 grams) frozen pineapple chunks
¼ teaspoon (1 gram) blue spirulina

To make the purple layer:

1. Place the banana, lime juice, and coconut milk in a blender. Blend until smooth.
2. Add the pineapple, blueberries, and blackberries. Blend until smooth. If the mixture is too thick, add additional coconut milk.
3. Split the drink between two large cups leaving about a quarter of the cup empty. Cover the glasses and place in the freezer until you make the other layers.

To make the yellow layer:

1. Clean out your blender. Place the banana, lemon zest and juice, lime zest and juice, and coconut milk in the blender. Blend until smooth.
2. Add the pineapple and citric acid. Blend until smooth.
3. Take one of the glasses with the purple layer and top with the yellow layer.

To make the blue layer:

1. Clean out your blender. Place the banana and coconut milk in the blender. Blend until smooth.
2. Add the pineapple and blue spirulina. Blend until smooth.
3. Take one of the glasses with the purple layer and top with the blue layer.

Centiskorch

Spicy Tropical Curry

This spicy tropical curry is full of beautiful colors and patterns to match Centiskorch, but it's important to practice good kitchen safety when frying the plantains. You would be careful around a Centiskorch's burning body, and you should be just as careful when working with hot oil in the kitchen.

Difficulty: ●●○○
Prep Time: 45 minutes
Cook Time: 1 hour
Yield: 4 to 6 servings
Dietary Notes: Vegan, gluten-free

Equipment: Medium saucepan with lid, large baking sheet, medium pot, medium nonstick pan, large bowl, small bowl

Saffron Rice

1 pinch saffron threads
¼ cup (59 milliliters) boiling water
2 tablespoons (30 milliliters) coconut oil
½ onion, minced
2 garlic cloves, minced
1¾ cups (585 grams) basmati rice
2 teaspoons (8 grams) kosher salt
3¾ cups (887 milliliters) vegetable broth

Curry

4 Yukon gold potatoes, cut into 2-inch pieces
2 carrots, cut into 2-inch pieces
4 baby portobello mushrooms, quartered
2 tablespoons (30 milliliters) olive oil
Kosher salt
Pepper
2 teaspoons (7 grams) garam masala
2 teaspoons (6 grams) cardamom
1 teaspoon (3 grams) ground turmeric
1 teaspoon (3 grams) paprika
1 teaspoon (3 grams) ground coriander
1 teaspoon (3 grams) ground cumin
1½ teaspoons (5 grams) Kashmiri chile powder
½ teaspoon (1 gram) ground cinnamon
2 tablespoons (30 milliliters) coconut oil
½ red onion, chopped
1 tablespoon (10 grams) garlic paste
1 tablespoon (10 grams) ginger paste
14 ounces (414 grams) crushed tomatoes
14 ounces (414 grams) tomato sauce
½ cup (118 milliliters) vegetable broth
2 tablespoons (20 grams) coconut sugar
⅔ cup (158 milliliters) coconut cream
3 plantains, very ripe
Peanut oil for frying

To make the saffron rice:

1. Place the saffron and boiling water in a cup and allow to steep for 5 minutes. Heat a medium saucepan with coconut oil over medium heat. Melt the coconut oil and add the onions and cook until translucent, about 5 minutes. Add the garlic and cook for another 2 minutes.
2. Add the rice and cook until slightly toasted, about 3 minutes. Add the saffron water, salt, and vegetable broth. Bring to a boil and then reduce the heat to low. Cover and cook until the rice has cooked, about 20 minutes.

To make the curry:

1. Preheat oven to 425°F (218°C). Bring a medium pot of water to a boil and add the potatoes and carrots. Cook for 8 minutes, or until slightly tender. Transfer the potatoes and carrots to a large bowl with mushrooms and olive oil. Place the oiled vegetables on a large baking sheet and sprinkle with salt and pepper. Bake for 20 minutes, toss, and bake for another 15 minutes, or until tender.
2. While the vegetables are roasting, combine the garam masala, cardamom, turmeric, paprika, coriander, cumin, chile powder, and cinnamon in a small bowl. Heat a medium pot with coconut oil over medium-high heat. Add the red onion and cook until translucent, about 5 minutes. Add the garlic and ginger paste and cook until fragrant, about 2 minutes. Add the spice mixture and mix until well combined.
3. Add the crushed tomatoes, tomato sauce, and vegetable broth. Mix well, making sure there are no clumps of spices left. Simmer for 15 minutes.
4. Add the coconut sugar and coconut cream. Taste and season with salt and pepper if needed. Add the roasted vegetables and lightly mix until combined.
5. Prepare the plantains by cutting them open and slicing into ½-inch-thick pieces and lightly salt. Fill a medium nonstick pan with ½ inch of peanut oil and heat over medium heat. Once heated, carefully add the plantains and cook each side until golden, about 2 to 3 minutes per side.
6. Transfer to a paper towel on a plate to drain excess oil off. Don't leave them on the paper towel for too long or they can get stuck. Serve warm.
7. To make a serving, place a portion of saffron rice on the plate and top with the curry. Place the plantains on top.

Clobbopus

Vanilla Punch

Clobbopus likes to punch its surroundings to explore, but you shouldn't do the same. You wouldn't want to break anything or hurt anyone! Better to enjoy your punch as a drink than to throw one.

Difficulty: ●○○○
Prep Time: 15 minutes
Yield: 1 serving
Dietary Notes: Vegetarian

Equipment: Ice cream scoop

1 scoop orange sherbet
2 scoops vanilla ice cream
8 fresh blueberries
½ cup (118 milliliters) orange soda
⅓ cup (79 milliliters) ginger ale

Place 1 scoop of orange sherbet into a large glass. Top with 2 scoops of vanilla ice cream. Add the blueberries. Pour in the orange soda and ginger ale. Serve with a spoon and straw to enjoy.

Morpeko Crêpes

These amazing lemon and berry crêpes look just like Morpeko's different colors! Did you know Morpeko gets into trouble when it's hungry? Be sure to eat your fill so you don't end up the same.

Difficulty: ●●●○
Prep Time: 45 minutes
Rest Time: 1 hour
Cook Time: 30 minutes
Yield: 6 to 10 servings
Dietary Notes: Vegetarian

Equipment: Medium saucepan, whisk, blender, fine mesh strainer, medium frying pan

Berry Curd

3 ounces (85 grams) fresh blueberries
4 ounces (113 grams) fresh blackberries
3 egg yolks
½ cup (110 grams) sugar
½ lemon, juiced
1 pinch kosher salt
¼ cup (56 grams) unsalted butter

Lemon Curd

3 egg yolks
½ cup (110 grams) sugar
1 tablespoon (6 grams) lemon zest
⅓ cup (79 milliliters) lemon juice
1 pinch kosher salt
¼ cup (56 grams) unsalted butter

Light Brown Crêpe

½ cup (77 grams) all-purpose flour
1 pinch ground cinnamon
½ cup plus 2 tablespoons (148 milliliters) milk
1 egg
2 tablespoons (28 grams) unsalted butter, melted and cooled
½ tablespoon (10 grams) honey
1 teaspoon (5 milliliters) vanilla extract
Nonstick cooking spray for greasing
Whipped cream for garnishing

Dark Chocolate Crêpe

1 cup (154 grams) all-purpose flour
2 tablespoons (18 grams) black cocoa powder
1¼ cups (296 milliliters) milk
2 eggs
¼ cup (56 grams) unsalted butter, melted and cooled
1 tablespoon (21 grams) honey
2 teaspoons (10 milliliters) vanilla extract

To make the berry curd:

1. Place the berries in a blender and blend until smooth. Pass through a fine mesh strainer. You want to end up with ⅓ to ½ cup of juice.

2. In a medium saucepan, whisk the egg yolks, sugar, and berry juice until the sugar dissolves and smooths. Add the lemon juice and salt. Place over low heat and whisk until it thickens, about 10 minutes.

3. Add the butter and whisk until the butter is completely melted. Strain into an airtight container and allow to cool completely. Place in the refrigerator for at least 1 hour before serving. The curd can be refrigerated for up to 1 week.

To make the lemon curd:

1. In a medium saucepan, whisk the egg yolks, sugar, and lemon zest until the sugar dissolves and smooths. Add the lemon juice and salt. Place over low heat and whisk until it thickens, about 10 minutes.

2. Add the butter. Whisk until the butter is completely melted. Strain into an airtight container and allow to cool completely. Place in the refrigerator for at least 1 hour before serving. The curd can be refrigerated for up to 1 week.

To make the light brown crêpe and dark chocolate crêpe:

1. To make the light brown crêpe: Place all the ingredients in a blender, except for the nonstick cooking spray and whipped cream, and blend until smooth. Transfer the batter into an airtight container and let rest in the refrigerator for at least 1 hour.

2. To make the dark chocolate crêpe: Repeat step 1 with all the chocolate crêpe ingredients.

3. Remove the crêpe batter from the refrigerator and give it a good mix. Begin heating a medium frying pan on medium heat. Spray the pan with nonstick cooking spray. Using a ladle, pour ¼ to ½ cup of batter onto the heated pan. Make sure to spread the batter around the frying pan so that the crêpe is nice and thin.

4. Cook the crêpe on one side for 3 to 5 minutes, or until it begins to brown. Carefully flip the crêpe and allow it to brown on the other side. Repeat with the remaining batter. Serve with the curds and whipped cream.

note: **If you prefer, lemon and berry curd can be purchased already made as well.**

Cufant

Thai Iced Tea Float

Cufant is super strong. It's able to carry over five tons! Fortunately, this delicious iced tea float doesn't weigh that much, so you'll be able to enjoy it without requiring a Cufant to lift it for you.

Difficulty: ●●○○
Prep Time: 30 minutes
Rest Time: 12 hours
Cook Time: 30 minutes
Yield: 6 to 8 drinks
Dietary Notes: Vegetarian

Equipment: Large pot, large pitcher, large bowl, medium bowl, whisk, stand mixer with whisk attachment

Thai Black Tea

4½ cups (1 liter) water
1 tablespoon (320 grams) coconut sugar
5 green cardamom pods, crushed
3 star anise pods
3 cloves
1 cinnamon stick
4 bags Ceylon tea
1 tablespoon (15 milliliters) vanilla extract

Vanilla Cardamom Ice Cream

14 ounces (396 grams) sweetened condensed milk
1 vanilla bean, seeds scraped and pod discarded
½ teaspoon (2 grams) ground cardamom
2 teaspoons (5 milliliters) vanilla extract
1 pinch kosher salt
2 cups (473 milliliters) heavy cream

Boba

5 cups (1,183 milliliters) water
½ cup (90 grams) instant black tapioca pearls
2 tablespoons (22 grams) coconut sugar
2 tablespoons (28 grams) brown sugar

Per Serving

Boba for garnishing
3 scoops vanilla cardamom ice cream
1 cup (237 milliliters) Thai black tea
¼ cup (59 milliliters) coconut milk
Orange food dye for coloring (optional)

To make the Thai black tea:

1. Combine the water, sugar, green cardamom pods, star anise, cloves, and cinnamon stick in a large pot. Heat over medium-high heat and bring to a boil. Reduce the heat and simmer for 15 minutes.

2. Remove from the heat, add the tea bags, cover, and let steep for 10 to 15 minutes. Strain into a large pitcher and add the vanilla extract. Allow to cool completely and then place in the refrigerator to chill. The tea can be stored in the refrigerator for up to 2 weeks.

To make vanilla cardamom ice cream:

1. Combine the sweetened condensed milk, vanilla bean seeds, cardamom, vanilla extract, and salt in a large bowl. Whisk together until well combined.

2. Place the heavy cream into a bowl of a stand mixer. Mix on medium-high speed until the whipped cream forms medium peaks, about 2 minutes. Transfer to the bowl with everything else. Carefully fold in the whipped cream until it is well combined.

3. Transfer to an airtight container and spread into a smooth even layer. Cover and place in the freezer for at least 5 hours before serving. This makes enough ice cream for 6 to 8 floats.

To make boba:

1. Place a large pot with water over medium-high heat. Bring to a boil and add the tapioca pearls. Stir and cook for 2 to 3 minutes, or until the pearls float.

2. Cover and reduce the heat to medium-low. Continue to cook for another 2 to 3 minutes.

3. Turn off the heat, keep covered, and cook for another 2 to 4 minutes, or until the tapioca has softened completely.

4. Drain through a strainer and rinse thoroughly with cold water.

5. Combine the sugars and ½ cup (118 milliliters) of hot water in a medium bowl. Whisk together until the sugar has dissolved. Add the tapioca and allow to rest for 10 minutes.

6. The boba can be stored in the refrigerator for up to 6 hours.

For assembly:

To make a serving, prepare a glass by placing boba on the bottom. Add the 3 scoops of ice cream. In another glass, combine the Thai black tea, coconut milk, and orange food dye. Mix together until combined. Pour into the glass with the ice cream and enjoy.

Dietary Considerations

Recipe	Page	Gluten-free	Nondairy	Vegan	Vegetarian
Abomasnow - Vichyssoise	65			X	X
Alolan Exeggutor - Tall Tropical Slushie	111			X	X
Ampharos - Lemonade	33			X	X
Bewear - Raspberry Chocolate Cupcakes	105				X
Breloom - Spring Rolls	47			X	X
Bruxish - Slush	109			X	X
Centiskorch - Spicy Tropical Curry	119	X		X	X
Charizard - Spicy Arrabbiata	17				X
Clobbopus - Vanilla Punch	121				X
Combee - Honey Cookies	57				X
Crustle - Parfaits	79				X
Cufant - Thai Iced Tea Float	125				X
Darumaka - Tomato Soup	77				X
Dedenne - Ramen	95				X
Dragonite - Butternut Squash Gnocchi	27				X
Drifloon - Blackberry Marshmallows	59				
Eldegoss - Spinach Mushroom Burger	115				X
Flygon - Avocado Toast	53				X
Froslass - Blackberry Ice Cream	67				X
Furret - Fluffy Pancakes	31				X
Gengar - Yogurt Bowl	23				X
Gogoat - Breakfast Burritos	89		X		X
Incineroar - Eggplant Parmigiana Sandwiches	101				X
Marshtomp - Umeboshi Onigiri	45			X	X
Miltank - Milk Bread	39				X
Morpeko - Crepes	123				X
Mudbray - Babka	103				X
Munchlax - Custard Bao	61				X
Musharna - Strawberry Taro Slush	73				X
Pancham - Rice Bowls	91			X	X
Pansage, Pansear, and Panpour - Roasted Cauliflower	71				X
Pikachu - Lemon Tart	19				X
Poké Ball Poke Bowls - Poké Ball	11		X		
Poké Ball Poke Bowls - Fast Ball	12		X		
Poké Ball Poke Bowls - Dusk Ball	12			X	X
Pyroar - Bruschetta	87			X	X
Relicanth - Chocolate Malt	53				X
Seaking - Dragon Fruit Agua Fresca	25			X	X
Shuckle - Berry Juice	33				X
Sliggoo - Purple Cauliflower Soup	97			X	X
Spinda - Raspberry Marble Cake	51				X
Stunfisk - Flatbreads	81				X
Swadloon - Tofu Lettuce Wraps	75			X	X
Swalot - Ube Flan	49				X
Swinub - Truffles	37				X
Sylveon - Strawberry Shortcake	93				X
Toxtricity - Yellow and Blue Smoothie	117			X	X
Tsareena - Roast Beet Salad	107	X			X
Umbreon - Dark Chocolate Bagels	35				X
Weavile - Ice Pops	65	X		X	X

About the Author

Victoria Rosenthal launched her blog, Pixelated Provisions, in 2012 to combine her lifelong passions for video games and food by recreating consumables found in many of her favorite games. When she isn't experimenting in the kitchen and dreaming up new recipes, she spends time with her husband and corgi hiking, playing video games, and enjoying the latest new restaurants. Victoria is also the author of *Fallout: The Vault Dweller's Official Cookbook*, *Destiny: The Official Cookbook*, *Street Fighter: The Official Street Food Cookbook*, and *The Ultimate FINAL FANTASY XIV Cookbook*. Feel free to say hello on Twitter, Twitch, or Instagram at PixelatedVicka.

INSIGHT EDITIONS

PO Box 3088
San Rafael, CA 94912
www.insighteditions.com

Find us on Facebook: www.facebook.com/InsightEditions
Follow us on Twitter: @insighteditions

Library of Congress Cataloging-in-Publication Data available.

Trade ISBN: 978-1-64722-662-6
Gift Set ISBN: 978-1-64722-755-5
Gamestop Edition: 978-1-64722-965-8
Gamestop Gift Set: 978-1-64722-964-1

Publisher: Raoul Goff
VP of Licensing and Partnerships: Vanessa Lopez
VP of Creative: Chrissy Kwasnik
VP of Manufacturing: Alix Nicholaeff
VP, Editorial Director: Vicki Jaeger
Managing Editor: Maria Spano
Senior Designer: Monique Narboneta Zosa
Senior Editor: Jennifer Sims
Associate Editor: Anna Wostenberg
Senior Production Editor: Elaine Ou
Production Associate: Deena Hashem
Senior Production Manager, Subsidiary Rights: Lina s Palma-Temena

ROOTS of PEACE REPLANTED PAPER
Insight Editions, in association with Roots of Peace, will plant two trees for each tree used in the manufacturing of this book. Roots of Peace is an internationally renowned humanitarian organization dedicated to eradicating land mines worldwide and converting war-torn lands into productive farms and wildlife habitats. Roots of Peace will plant two million fruit and nut trees in Afghanistan and provide farmers there with the skills and support necessary for sustainable land use.

Manufactured in China by Insight Editions

10 9 8 7 6 5 4 3 2 1